The Plastic-Free Gardener

Fairlight Books

Contents

Plastic in the Natural Environment

More and more scientists are reporting on the growing problem of plastic pollution in the world's natural environment: in our waterways and oceans, in the soil where we grow our food, and even in our food supplies.

Discarded or accidentally lost in the natural environment, plastics erode, breaking down into smaller and smaller pieces as wind, rain and sun take their toll. Over years, decades and even centuries, a piece of plastic will disintegrate into chunks, then fragments, and then tiny particles called *microplastics* and even smaller ones called *nanoplastics*.

It sounds like a natural process, but is far from it. Before plastics were mass produced in the 1950s, most things we would have used in the garden (that weren't made of metal or rock) would have naturally biodegraded. They were decomposed by bacteria and other living organisms until they became assimilated back into nature.

But commercially used plastic is not biodegradable. There is no living organism that is capable of biologically breaking down these chemically manufactured oil-based polymers. Instead of biodegrading, plastic erodes into smaller and smaller pieces, sometimes over hundreds of years, slowly leaching out the chemicals used in their manufacture. Although now banned from use, legacy plastics still in the environment continue to leach the carcinogenic chemicals polychlorinated biphenyls (PCBs) and polycyclic aromatic hydrocarbons (PAHs).

In the oceans, the broken-down plastic particles are ingested into the bodies of invertebrates, fish and other sea life, where they travel from intestinal tracts into tissue. Because fishmeal is used for animal and aquaculture feed, micro- and nanoplastic particles eventually end up in human food supplies. A 2021 study in *Nature Scientific Report*s that reviewed recent scientific research on the topic concluded that fishmeal does directly expose organisms intended for human consumption to microplastic particles.[1] Scientists are only now beginning to study the implications of this on human health.[2]

It's a world-wide problem. Microplastics are found in snails off the coast of Florida and in sea-floor sediment off the shore of the Maldives.[3] A study by Flinders University found the microplastics of synthetic polyamides (PAs), polyethylenes (PEs), polypropylenes (PPs), acrylic resin and polyethylene terephthalates (PETs) in common blue mussels across Southern Australia.[4]

And the problem isn't just restricted to the oceans. In the UK, a recent study by Cardiff University tracked the deposit of a range of microplastics onto farmlands via fertilisers derived from sewage sludge.[5]

In my own garden, I find little bits of plastic everywhere – fragments of food

WEEDING OUT PLASTIC

STRIMMER WITH PLASTIC CORD

and sweet wrappers blown in as litter, scraps of old plastic bags, pieces of synthetic string, refuse sacks, plastic ties, shards of hard plastic chipped off watering cans, leaf catchers and propagators that have become tatty from exposure to UV rays or just general wear... the list goes on.

I even find fragments and particles mixed in with the soil and compost that I've bought and actually dug into my garden's flower and vegetable beds. The scraps in the soil derive from the processing of farm, kitchen and garden waste contaminated by plastic.

The problem is that unless we've had a 'plastic epiphany', it's so easy to not see plastic, or at least not to see it for the issue that it is. So it ends up everywhere.

Have you ever used a strimmer with a plastic cord to trim weeds, and wondered what happened to the cord? After a while, it seems to just disappear and needs to be replaced. Well, the cord doesn't fall out and get lost. Over time, as the strimmer is used, it is sliced into thousands of tiny pieces which are sprinkled onto the land and into the vegetation. When you think about it for long enough, it seems unbelievable that this is how the product is designed to operate.

PLASTICS IN THE OCEAN

When people consider plastic pollution, they usually think first of the issue of plastic in the oceans – the Pacific Ocean in particular.

The 'Great Pacific Garbage Patch' is the name given to a floating mountain of plastic debris that has accumulated in two great swirls of currents, one between Hawaii and California and the other between Hawaii and Japan. These floating garbage patches are made up of all sorts of plastic items: bottles, toothbrushes, fishing ropes, carrier bags and so on.

A review in *Nature* modelled data from multi-vessel and aircraft surveys inside an area of 1.6 million square kilometres, and estimated that around 79,000 metric tons of plastic were floating there. They also found that the amount of plastic in the area was rapidly accumulating.[6]

Where does it all come from? Well, much of it comes from debris discarded over years by fishing industries, but there are myriad other ways in which plastics end up in our marine environment – through clothes made of synthetic fibres being washed; through milk cartons, drinking bottles and sweet wrappers being blown or thrown into the sea; through synthetic personal care products being released with raw sewage.

It's been estimated that between 4.8 and 12.7 million metric tons of plastic waste enter the ocean from the land every year.[7] This is on top of the many tons of plastic-based debris that was regularly discarded by fishing industries around the world before consideration was given to the longer-term impact of that practice.

The thought of thousands of tons of plastic debris floating in the middle of the ocean is shocking, but it's actually only part of the problem. As the plastic disintegrates into smaller pieces from the effect of the sun and ocean winds, the pieces start to sink and spread out. The majority of the plastic fragments in the ocean are far smaller in size than those pieces that can be seen in the Great Pacific Garbage Patch and are much more widely dispersed. Scientists can only guess how much of the plastic in the oceans has sunk to the bottom, and what size the pieces might be. One article in *National Geographic* estimated that 8% of the tonnage of plastics in the Great Pacific Garbage Patch is made up of the tiniest microplastic particles, and the extent of microplastic pollution in the ocean as a whole is still largely unknown.[8]

IS RECYCLING THE ANSWER?

In a dream world, all plastic would be recaptured after use and recycled into new products in one great eternal cycle. Unfortunately, this is far from the case, even where we try as hard as we can to recycle all our plastics correctly.

Globally, 18% of plastics are recycled and 24% are incinerated, while more than half, – 58% – are sent to landfill or lost in the natural environment.[9]

In most developed countries, recyclable waste is collected kerbside by the local authorities who pass it to waste disposal companies. The disposal companies might do one of three things. They might incinerate it. In this case, at least the plastic does not end up in the natural environment. They might recycle it. Or, if processing facilities are at capacity, they might send it to landfill. Of the share targeted for recycling, a vast proportion of recycling from the west is shipped to recycling facility providers in other countries.

Before 2016, more than half of the 3.91 million metric tons of plastics collected each year in the US was shipped abroad.[10] Much of that went to China, but after China refused to accept any more contaminated plastics in late 2017, the US increasingly started to send its waste to countries that do not have modern waste-management facilities, instead using manual labour to process it. There are reports of waste from the US being shipped to Bangladesh, Laos, Ethiopia and Senegal.[11]

It's a similar situation in the UK. In 2020, recycling waste from the UK went to Malaysia, Pakistan, Vietnam, Indonesia and Turkey.[12]

Each time recycling waste is sold on there is a new opportunity for it to be lost into the environment, and there is less chance it will be recycled and more chance it will end up in landfill or on garbage dumps waiting to be sorted by hand.

When we pass plastics to our local authority, they meet their recycling target and we feel we have done our bit, even if the waste is actually just sold on. When we put a bit of plastic in our recycling bin, we don't really know where it will end up. The 'out of sight, out of mind' mentality is one of the biggest problems.

Even for plastic that does end up recycled, this isn't a perfect solution. Much of plastic recycling is what Lucy Siegle calls 'downcycling' in her brilliant book *Turning the Tide on Plastic*.[13] Plastic bottles, which make up a huge proportion of the plastic that can be recycled, are converted into plastic flakes or pellets and sold to other manufacturers. Many of these flakes are bought by manufacturers to make synthetic clothes, but synthetic fibres themselves cannot be recycled, so the clothes must be put into the normal rubbish when discarded, from which they will be sent to landfill. Much of the textile waste from consumers in the US ends up in landfill in Chile and West Africa.[14]

So the recycling of plastic is not exactly an eternal cycle of renewal but often just a single makeover before the product is sent off to landfill, to the incinerator, or to developing nations to be processed.

RECYCLED METAL TINS

WAKING UP TO PLASTIC

Since we started producing plastic in industrial quantities, it has worked its way into nearly every aspect of our lives. It serves wonderful, life-saving purposes, providing medical solutions that wouldn't be possible without it. The fact that it is light means when used in the manufacture of motor vehicles, it reduces the carbon emissions compared to earlier materials used.

It's convenient as a packaging material: it keeps products clean, and stops them getting damaged or water-spoiled when travelling through the supply chain from the manufacturer to us.

In the aisles of most supermarkets, it's not uncommon still to see nothing but wall-to-wall plastic packaging. A lot of plastic packaging doesn't even look or feel like plastic – crisp packets, shiny foil chocolate and sweet wrappers, orange string used to bundle up fruit. The same can be said of other plastic products, such as teabags made of plastic or soft acrylic jumpers. There's a long list of plastic packaging or fabrics that have been made to look like natural materials. Or else the plastic wrapping is hidden inside a natural-looking cardboard box. It's estimated that over one third of plastics are produced for use as packaging materials.[15]

In the garden centre, a place where we are shopping for things to bring into our own little piece of nature, plastic is everywhere: in pots, netting, cloches, fleeces, watering cans, landscaping fabric, string, clips, sprays, hoses, seed trays... and that's before you start looking at the packaging.

Plastic is cheap, tough and durable, so like an invasive weed it has become the dominant material used in the manufacture of consumer goods, pushing out our native, or natural, materials: glass, wood, wool, cotton, paper, wicker. But it is precisely this durability that is the problem.

We might touch a piece of plastic packaging for just a moment or two, but it will then be around for hundreds of years. It will be breaking down into smaller and smaller pieces, forming durable scraps and microplastic particles, and potentially finding its way into the natural environment and the food chain centuries later.

MY OWN PLASTIC EPIPHANY

Before I had my own 'plastic epiphany', I was completely blind to plastics. I would recycle where I could, but wouldn't give a thought to throwing single-use or unrecyclable plastic into the waste bin.

Then something happened that made me stop and think.

Over lockdown, like many others, I created a vegetable patch in my garden. It was small for a vegetable plot – around three square metres – and I really enjoyed setting it up and managing it. I was surprised by how much delicious produce it provided even though I hadn't grown vegetables for many years.

That first year I had carrots, spring onions, pink fir potatoes, sweet gem lettuce, dwarf beans, coriander, rocket, cherry tomatoes, pak choi and courgettes. It wasn't all plain sailing – my strawberries were stolen by mice, my sprouting broccoli was infested by bugs and some of my tomato plants went rotten at their base – but overall, it was a great success. So the next year, I decided to expand it.

The original patch was made up of three long beds separated with paths con- structed according to a fairly standard method. It had a base of plastic groundsheet, cut to size to act as a weed barrier and covered with bark to deter slugs. The paths served their purpose well over the year, but the edges became mired in the soil of the beds and decomposed pieces of bark.

The next year, when I lifted the first strip of plastic groundsheet and tried to peel it away from where it was embedded in the earth, I discovered the woven edges had started to fray. Big strips of plastic were unravelling and coming loose as I lifted it. At the time, I didn't really think too much about it, just scooped them up and tucked them into a pot to go in the bin.

Later that afternoon I saw that my dog was fretting at her paw. On closer inspection, I found she had some of that frayed plastic strip wrapped around her leg. It was pretty tight and I had to get scissors to cut it off. I went back to search for any other plastic strips that I might have missed. As I did so, I worried that any leftover loose strips blowing about might get wrapped around the leg of one of the wild animals who visit the garden. I fretted that the strips might be a hazard to wildlife for some years to come.

How many years might it be? Would the plastic eventually biodegrade or somehow wear away to nothing? When I got back in, I searched the internet to find out and was shocked by the result. The woven plastic strips were probably made of polypropylene (PP), and would never biodegrade. To degrade, which seemed to mean to slowly wear away to nothing, would take over two hundred years.

Two hundred years! I thought of all the generations of squirrels, deer, moles, foxes, birds and rabbits who live in and around my garden, and who might be affected over the next two centuries if I didn't catch all the frayed pieces of groundsheet.

It made me start to think about the mountain of plastic I had used in my life and wonder how much of it might still be around. Looking into it further, I discovered there was a pretty good chance that at least some of the plastic I had used would have ended up in the natural environment, and that a good proportion of the rest was probably still buried in landfill, in much the same shape as the day it was discarded.

The trouble is that the 'system' is set up to ensure that we never have to see the mountain of non-biodegradable waste that we create. It's not like we walk out the front door and put the sweet wrapper or crisp packet on a pile in the street.

Imagine if it were the case. Imagine a mountain of non-biodegradable plastic sitting outside each house, growing daily.

Instead, we have developed a system that allows us to turn a blind eye to it. The plastic we might use for ten seconds of our lives, dispose of and instantly forget is conveniently absent. This is one of the biggest barriers to change that we all face as consumers of plastic: we have set up a system that allows us to turn a blind eye to the consequences of our lifestyles of convenience.

Reflecting on the strips of frayed plastic groundsheet, and beginning to see plastic in a new light, I decided to make a change to my lifestyle.

I trialled a month living entirely plastic-free. It was remarkably difficult. However, the process helped me to scrutinise how invasive plastic was in my and my family's lifestyle and helped us to discover ways to change our habits. My plastic consumption was not entirely eradicated, but it was significantly reduced. For household use, my consumption of recyclable plastic fell by around 50%, and that of single-use and unrecyclable plastic by around 80%.

However, I was determined that for the garden, I would aim for 100% plastic free.

WHAT EXACTLY IS PLASTIC?

Most plastics are chemically engineered from fossil fuels such as oil or natural gas. Classed as synthetic polymers, they are made of long strings of complex molecules which do not chemically change when subjected to heat, meaning they can be moulded into a vast array of shapes. Different arrangements of the polymer molecules will create different sorts of plastic: those that are hard and robust, those that are soft and flexible, those that can be drawn out into a pliable yet strong cord, or those that can be teased into a soft thread and then woven or pressed into fabric. They can be silvered to look like foil or pumped full of air to create strong insulating bricks. They are waterproof, and have a fantastic strength-to-weight ratio. In many ways, plastics are a miracle product, but they have been over-manufactured to such an extent that their longevity and durability are greater than necessary.

With so many different types of plastic, it's often difficult to look at a plastic product or piece of packaging and know whether it is recyclable or not. In the US and the UK, retailers have come a long way in making sure that packaging, particularly food packaging, has clear labels giving guidance on recycling. But unfortunately this is not the case for garden products. When you walk around many garden centres, it's still pretty hard to figure out what type of plastic the products on the shelves are made of and harder still to tell whether they or the packaging they come in are recyclable. Buying online is no different – many products just have a label that describes them as made of 'plastic'.

So, any effort to reduce single-use plastic, or to cut down on unrecyclable plastic, can be challenging without a good understanding of the different types of plastic used in gardening products.

Resin Identification Code (RIC)	Polymer	Uses
[1] PET	Polyethylene terephthalate (PET)	One of the most common types of plastic, polyethylene terephthalate (PET) is extensively used in a hard moulded form for soft drinks bottles, and woven into a fabric, such as polyester, for the manufacture of synthetic clothes.
		In the garden, it is used to create seed trays and propagators, and in a flexible form for garden waste buckets.
		Drink bottles can be widely recycled, usually into plastic pellets ready for the manufacture of new products. Where the pellets are used to make synthetic clothing, the cycle ends. They cannot, currently, be readily recycled beyond that.
		Some recycling facilities accept hard PET products, but most are unable to recycle garden plastics because of soil contamination.
		It is estimated that a solid PET bottle in landfill takes around 450 years to degrade. Synthetic clothes take between 20 and 200 years depending on the form of the fibre used.
[2] HDPE	High-density polyethylene (HDPE or PE-HD)	The high-density polyethylene (HDPE) polymer is very tough, so when moulded into shape it is used for consumer items that need to be strong. You'll recognise it in plastic chairs and toys, milk cartons, jerry cans and bottle crates.
		It can be woven into a plastic fibre for rope and synthetic clothing, and it can be stretched to a strong, fine film and moulded into cheap, disposable shopping bags.
		Because it doesn't break down easily, even when exposed to UV rays or extreme cold and heat, it has been considered by manufacturers to be an ideal material for garden products.
		In its many forms it is found in: rigid plant pots (mostly coloured black, brown and green); seed trays; containers for liquid feeds, pesticides, herbicides and fertilisers; insect-proof mesh; wheelbarrows; garden seating; and leaf grabbers.
		Theoretically, HDPE materials can be recycled, but most processing plants can only accept it in its harder form, without soil contamination, and cannot accept black-coloured plastic pots.
		It takes around 500 years for HDPE to degrade.

Resin Identification Code (RIC)	Polymer	Uses
3 PVC	Polyvinyl chloride (PVC)	In a flexible yet strong form, polyvinyl chloride (PVC) is used for electrical cabling and rope. It is also moulded into shape for a huge range of products such as building materials, windows, flooring, seat coverings and shoes. In the garden, some hosepipes are made of PVC (often mixed with rubber), and it is used to make moulded seed trays and cloches. PVC is not widely recycled. It is estimated to take around 450 years to degrade.
4 LDPE	Low-density polyethylene (LDPE or PE-LD)	Easily moulded into complex shapes, low-density polyethylene (LDPE) is used to make tubing, parts for machines, plastic bags, and – in a form everyone would recognise – as rings for six-packs. It's also used to make some juice and milk cartons, and for the super-stretchy plastic wrap (or cling film) used in the kitchen. In the garden, you'll find it used to make plant containers and bags to hold soil and compost. Theoretically, LDPE can be recycled, but most waste processing plants will not recycle the softest types of LDPE such as plastic wrap, or soil-contaminated compost bags. It is estimated that LDPE takes 500 years to degrade.
5 PP	Polypropylene (PP)	Like many other polymer types, polypropylene (PP) is flexible and strong, but it is also extremely heat-resistant, so is used for goods which take a lot of wear and tear, such as carpets and doormats, and for items which are exposed to heat, such as dishwasher-proof kitchenware. It is also used in a softer material form for nappies, sanitary products and thermal clothing. In the garden, you will find it used for plant pots, some compost and soil bags, clear cloches and fleece to keep plants free of frost, and woven into synthetic twine. In some forms it can be recycled, but otherwise it takes between 200 and 450 years to degrade.

Resin Identification Code (RIC)	Polymer	Uses
	Polystyrene (PS)	For the packaging industry, polystyrene (PS) is heaven-sent. For our purposes, it is very much the opposite, and falls squarely into the 'ugly' category of plastics.
		In the form of a block of granules pumped full of air and moulded into the required shape, it is a robust and incredibly light packaging material – but unpack a plant or garden implement that has arrived in it, and pretty soon there will be little beads of polystyrene flying off into the ether. They become static and cling to surfaces with some strange elusive magnetism, refusing to be swept up or contained.
		Polystyrene also comes in a hard form that might be seen, for example, in the casings of smoke detectors and moulded into disposable razors.
		For the garden, polystyrene arrives usually as packaging material, particularly for electric tools, but also for breakable or fragile items, such as glass products and plants.
		Theoretically, polystyrene can be recycled, but most forms are not accepted for recycling, including the aerated packaging blocks.
		Those little beads of polystyrene which fly off, never to be seen again? They are estimated to take more than 500 years to degrade.
None	Polyurethane (PUR)	A slightly different beast, polyurethane is created by reacting two chemical compounds (an isocyanate and a polyol), rather than being synthesised from fossil fuels.
		Softer and not quite as durable as other plastics, you would typically recognise it as the material bathroom sponges are made of. Polyurethanes are also used for the manufacture of the soles of shoes, surfboards, car seats and water tanks, acting as a sealant, an adhesive and a plastic laminate that looks like varnish.
		In the garden, it might be used for knotted string bird netting, or as a fine mesh for bug netting. It is sometimes used in the manufacture of garden hosing and for the rubber-like strips on the handles of tools.
		Not having the same durability as petroleum-based plastics, it is quicker to degrade, taking around twenty to thirty years.

BIOPLASTICS

When it comes to plastic packaging, it's worth remembering that 'degradable' is not the same as 'biodegradable'.

Most things in nature are biodegradable, which means that over time they are decomposed by bacteria or other living organisms until they disappear to nothing – part of the perpetual cycle of nature. Plastics are not biodegradable; there is no living organism that can digest them. Instead, they degrade, breaking into smaller and smaller particles of the same plastic polymer. As we saw from the table, this process can take up to five hundred years. It can then take several hundred more for the polymer chemicals to mineralise back into natural organic compounds.

There is a form of packaging called 'bioplastic' which is increasingly used as a plastic alternative, particularly in the food industry. Usually made from corn starch, it is clear and has a distinctive soft, almost sticky feel to it. It biodegrades over time in a natural way, and should be placed in the food waste or general waste after use. Unless it says that it is home-compostable, it is best not to put it on the compost heap, as it can take too long to biodegrade. It should never be placed in the plastic recycling waste as that can compromise the recycling.

Bioplastic is a great alternative to plastic packaging, but unfortunately it is not commonly used to package gardening products. Perhaps over time, and with enough consumer demand, it will be.

BIODEGRADABLE GLOVES

WHAT DOES 'DEGRADE' ACTUALLY MEAN?

It's impossible to find clear or consistent figures for how long different types of plastic polymers take to degrade, so the figures given in the table are all estimates. There are a few different reasons for this.

The first is that large-scale plastic manufacturing has only been in place for around seventy years, whereas most of the plastic polymers in commercial use take centuries to degrade. Scientists can only study degradation rates in certain environments and then extrapolate from that to estimate the likely time for a product to degrade when it is buried at the bottom of landfill.

Secondly, the rate of degradation will vary according to how much light and heat the discarded plastic product is exposed to. The degradation rate will also be influenced by which chemicals were added to the plastic to strengthen it during manufacture. Plastics will degrade much faster when floating in the ocean, where they are exposed to UV rays from the sun and buffeted by currents, than they will buried in the ground. Together these factors might alter the degradation rate of, say, a plastic bottle from a few decades to several hundred years.

And there's one last complication. These figures are based on studies measuring and extrapolating how long it would take for a piece of plastic to fragment and break down into smaller and smaller pieces until nothing visible is left, just microplastic or nanoplastic particles.

But there is a further stage of degradation, which is the mineralisation of the long, complex chain molecules of the plastic polymer back into naturally occurring compounds such as water and carbon dioxide. This process can take over a thousand years for some types of plastic.

Added together, these reasons explain why it is so hard to pin down consistent figures indicating whether a plastic bottle of water takes a few decades or a thousand years to finally degrade away to nothing.

But for us in the garden, the simple answer is that nearly all plastics that we use or allow to escape into the garden will outlive us and, in many cases, even generations that follow us.

'DEGRADABLE' AND 'FABRIC' GREENWASH

It is worth being careful of a little confusion that creeps in through 'greenwashing', meaning companies using marketing to appear more climate-friendly than they truly are.

One example is the use of the label 'degradable' on plastic wrapping and plastic bags.

All plastics are degradable – it can just take a thousand years to happen! So, putting the word 'degradable' on a plastic product or packaging means nothing; it just sounds a bit like 'biodegradable'. Obviously, the retailers are hoping consumers might buy it mistakenly thinking it is a form of bioplastic, which is biodegradable.

Another thing to watch out for is plant pots labelled as made of 'fabric', which are actually made of synthetic polyethylene terephthalate (PET) fibres. This is just a soft form of plastic that has been made to look like wool.

There are some great bioplastic and wool products out there, so if you are looking for a wool product, be sure you are getting the real thing.

How long does it take different types of plastic to degrade?[16]

Plastic bag – 20 years

Coffee cup – 30 years

Plastic straw – 200 years

Plastic rings (from can six-packs) – 400 years

Plastic water bottle – 450 years

Coffee pod – 500 years

Disposable nappy – 500 years

Plastic toothbrush – 500 years

The Good, the Bad and the Ugly

Working in the garden in a 100% plastic-free way can be tough. As seen in the table, plastics work their way into every aspect of gardening: the pots that plants are sold in; the handles of tools; the packaging our orders arrive in; the mesh and fleece we use to protect our plants from pests and harsh weather; the string and clips we use to tie them in.

Plastic seems to be irredeemably threaded through the gardening process. Even with my best endeavours to be plastic-free in the garden, plastic creeps in or compromises are made: products that arrive with unexpected plastic packaging, plant feed for which you can't find a ready alternative, tools which are largely plastic-free but have pieces of plastic in their make-up, or the gift of a plant delivered in a plastic pot.

Rather than be entirely plastic-free, if your aim is to reduce the amount of plastic you use and to be certain that none of it escapes into the natural environment, choices will need to be made. In which case, it's worth considering the good, the bad and the ugly of plastics in the garden.

THE GOOD

Obviously, in a book about plastic-free gardening, no plastics are 'good'. But if you are trying to make sure plastics do not end up escaping into the garden and that you recycle as much as you can of what you do use, let's start here. Perhaps this section should really be called 'not as bad as the rest'.

Into this category, let's put those plastics which might provide a lengthy service, perhaps for several generations, and which don't flake off into the environment. They might already be in your garden so you will keep using them – they will only go to landfill or be incinerated otherwise. These include birdfeeders, hosepipes, old plant pots, tools with plastic parts and wheelbarrows.

For example, I've had the same plastic wheelbarrow for about twenty years. I inherited it from the owners of our last house. It's still in perfectly good working order, so there doesn't seem any point in sending it to landfill. The same goes for a collection of bird feeders which have moulded plastic parts and which support a number of breeding species.

Some plant retailers offer plants in recyclable grey pots – these can also be put in this category.

THE BAD

Now for the bad. Into this category go all those plastic items which might be useful for one, two or even a few years, but which, when worn out, must be discarded into general waste rather than recycled.

They might be made of one of the unrecyclable polymers (for example, synthetic polyethylene terephthalate (PET) fleecy fibres or polypropylene (PP) synthetic mesh). They might be made from a form of a polymer that local recycling facilities cannot process because the plastic is too dark. Traditionally plant pots were made of black plastic because it allows the roots to have the darkest environment in which to grow, ensuring they are not deterred from growing towards the side of the pot. However, recycling processing machines use infrared detection systems to identify plastic and blow it into bins for processing. Black plastic absorbs the infrared and so passes by undetected. Finally, much garden plastic cannot be recycled by the usual household collection points because of dirt contamination.

Under this 'bad' category fall the cracked unrecyclable pots, the torn netting, the split, coloured seed trays, the worn synthetic gloves, the chipped leaf catchers, the broken hosepipe connectors, and most compost and soil bags.

This category also includes all the single use, unrecyclable plastics commonly used to package gardening products: in particular, polypropylene (PP) strapping, low-density polyethylene (LDPE) film and high-density polyethylene (HDPE) moulded trays.

WOVEN PLASTIC MEMBRANE

The great news is that, for most of the plastic products mentioned above, there are lots of plastic-free solutions. And the number of retailers who are focusing on supplying products without plastic packaging grows by the day. Larger garden centres often now have a section that provides some plastic-free solutions, and there are a host of smaller online retailers who focus on offering plastic-free garden products. Check out the directory at the end for some great examples.

THE UGLY

For me, the worst forms of plastic to use in the garden or on the vegetable patch are those that end up escaping into the natural environment, despite all attempts to avoid this.

Into the 'ugly' category fall those plastics that chip, disintegrate, flake off or get lost in the garden: woven strips of polypropylene (PP) ground-cover membrane that separate and fly away; torn ends of disintegrating polypropylene (PP) and polyurethane (PUR) fleeces; beads of polystyrene (PS) block packaging that refuse to be swept up and instead disappear off in the slightest breeze.

Let's also add products that are lost into the vegetation: rubbery green low-density polyethylene (LDPE) encased garden wire that is nibbled to nothing by wildlife; coloured polypropylene (PP) twine; and the 'invisible' green plastic clips used to tie up plants.

We can also add those plastics that are built into the natural environment during landscaping projects: pond liners, synthetic fabric laid beneath patios, and low-density polypropylene (LDPE) sheeting used to line earth beds.

For me, the prize for the worst offender goes to the electric strimmer with plastic blades or lines. As it is used, its line slowly erodes, strewing into the landscape tens of thousands of plastic pieces so tiny they will never be recovered.

If, like me, your garden has plastic pollution from all or any of these sources, there is not much that can be done other than to scrub it up where and when we can. But it's easy to make a change to prevent it happening in the future.

The good news is that there are alternatives for all of these plastic garden items – for example, choosing natural twine over plastic string, and plain metal ties over those encased in plastic. Sometimes you do have to be a bit inventive, but there is some fun in that too.

COLOURFUL JUTE TWINE

Getting Started

The best gardeners are organised, planning what they are going to plant and where they will source the plants well in advance. The same is doubly true for the plastic-free gardener.

One January, when I was new to gardening, I asked a green-fingered friend when I should plant my tulip bulbs for a gorgeous spring display. He scratched his head and said, 'Last October...?'

When trying to be plastic-free, whether for the household or the garden, the old saying 'to fail to prepare is to prepare to fail' really is true. A bit of upfront investment of time before the growing season works wonders towards ensuring a year of plastic-free gardening lies ahead.

If we get organised, we can figure out a plastic-free growing plan which includes: how to source seeds and plants; how to determine frost-protection solutions to extend the season at both ends; how to protect our growing plants from pests; how to feed our plants; and how to secure them in place as they grow – all without resorting to plastic.

FIRST STEPS

For the new gardener, growing from seed is a great way of obtaining a wide variety of flowers, herbs and vegetables in your garden, but you can also buy plants in plastic-free pots once you know where to source them.

In the UK, Kirton Farm Nurseries specialises in growing cottage garden plants and herbs in eco-friendly, sustainable coir pots. They don't sell to retail consumers, but in the UK you can find their plants in garden centres under the brand name The Hairy Pot Plant Company, so named because of the distinctive 'hairy' look of the coir pots. Their stock is wide, including a large range of plants for the herbaceous border and a good selection of herbs. You can find a list of retailers who stock their plants in the UK on their website, and a few of their larger distributors are listed in the directory at the back of this book. You can plant their flowers and herbs straight into the ground along with the coir pot, but I think they do better if you gently remove the pot. If you are careful with storage, they can then be reused for potting up seedlings the following year.

There are also now some nurseries that offer to remove the plastic pot at the point of sale, and will then reuse it. Others are starting to send plants purchased online without any plastic packaging and some are using cardboard pots designed specifically for the purpose, like POSIpots.

But growing from seed is still a fantastic way for a plastic-free gardener to ensure they can have a varied range of flowers, herbs and vegetables in their garden.

To sow seed early in the season, you don't need to have a greenhouse – a sunny windowsill or table reserved inside the house will do the job just as well. And many vegetable seeds, such as those of carrots, spring onions, sugar snap peas, mangetout, lettuce, spinach and pak choi, as well as many flower seeds, including cosmos, marigolds and wallflowers, can be sown directly into the ground where they will grow.

When starting seedlings off in the house or greenhouse, there are heaps of alternatives to the plastic seed trays and small pots that seem to dominate the market, such as pots and seed trays made from coconut coir, wood pulp fibre, bamboo, wood, metal and rubber.

For a lengthy flower- or vegetable-growing season, it is important to consider the best way to protect seedlings from early spring frosts as the frost-protection, the marketplace is also saturated by plastic fleeces and cloches.

For a splendid flower display, that will last for several years, consider planting bulbs or rhizomes. There are many that will fill the garden with wonderful colour through the spring and summer, and which can often be bought plastic-free in some garden centres or direct from some nurseries. Check the directory at the back for details.

Essentials

Seeds

Wood, bamboo or metal seed trays

Cardboard, fibre or rubber tube trainers

Coir, fibre, bamboo, husk, wool, metal or terracotta pots

Waterproof metal or bamboo trays

Metal watering can

Potting compost or coir pellets

Hand trowel

Spade

Wood, slate or bamboo seed markers

Natural twine

Scissors

Bamboo canes

Large jute bag

Good to Have

Metal gardening sieve

One or more glass panes

Biodegradable pest netting

Small or long-handled hoe

Glass cloches for vegetables

Large fork

EASY FLOWERS TO START WITH

Perennials

Anemone – A versatile little plant, happy in a pot, a lightly shaded bed or in full sun, Japanese anemones flower from a clump that grows in the spring, providing a host of very delicate, exceedingly pretty flowers in pinks and whites in late summer to early autumn. Once established they need little care, and will die back in winter ready to flower again the following year. Protect their base with a mulch over a cold winter.

Aster – These autumnal stars carry the flower garden through the late end of summer and into autumn, getting going just as most other flowering plants have died away for the year. The commonest form is lilac with a yellow polka dot centre, but they come in pink and white too. They are robust, prolific bloomers and will grow tall – some varieties even up to six feet.

Aubrieta – A small shrub with lots of little flowers that, once established in the garden, will spread happily through a rockery, clinging vertically on rough walls and needing zero supervision. The classic is a deep purple colour, but they are also available in white, pink, red and a delicate pastel blue.

Erigeron (fleabane) – Forming clumps of tiny pink and white daisy-like flowers, fleabane self-seeds along the gaps of stone walls and in the corners of any empty bed. Once established it needs no maintenance at all, but keeps on giving throughout the summer season.

Erysimum (wallflower) – These cheery blooms of red, orange, pink and yellow brighten up any garden with a riot of colour. Use either the biennials for spring bedding, or choose a perennial which will flower profusely through the summer.

Euphorbia and *Hellebore* – The perfect late winter, early spring combo for colour in shady areas beneath trees. Yellow or greenish-white, and rust-coloured respectively, once established both plants will gently spread at an even pace, but are easily managed and can be cut back if they have spread too far.

Geranium – The bee-attracting purple and lavender-blue varieties Rozanne and Johnson's Blue are much loved, and once established will flower profusely through the summer. (NB: these 'hardy' perennials are not to be confused with the annual with orange and red flowers that look so great in terracotta pots. Those are also marketed as 'geraniums', but are actually pelargoniums. See 'annuals' section for details.)

Helianthemum (rock rose) – A shrub that will happily make itself at home in a dry sunny border. It comes in a wide variety of colours from red, pink and orange to white. The contrast of its bright flowers against the soft green of its leaves is a delight.

Lavandula (lavender) – An aromatic bee magnet, with spikes of blue-purple flowers, which looks attractive with several plants merging to form a border edge. It prefers a sunny, well-drained position, but once established will last for many years, just needing the flowers' stalks to be cut back at the end of the summer.

Nepeta (catmint) – The purple spires of this flowering bush quickly fill up a border with thick blocks of colour and a lovely aroma. It requires little maintenance, yet flowers for weeks through the summer.

Perovskia (Russian sage) – A delicately showy plant, with feathery purple fronds, it looks impressive but is very easy to grow if given a sunny spot. Leave the dead stems over winter – they provide an architectural structure with their white fronds – and instead cut them back to the live base of the plant in spring, followed by a mulch. Great for bees.

Primula (primrose) – Either in their wild, yellow form, or the commercial variety of modified colours, primroses love clay soil, and will spread in clumps around the garden either on their own or with a helping hand through division in autumn or in late spring after they have flowered.

Rosa (rose) – From the perfect Valentine blooms of the tea rose to the delightful chaos of the rambler, there is a rose to suit every garden. Choose an award-winning, disease-resistant, repeat-flowering variety and you can't go too far wrong.

Salvia – The hardy herbaceous perennial salvias, like *Salvia x sylvestris*, form clump-like bushes that need little care, but the half-hardy varieties such as *Salvia greggii* are more eye-catching. So long as they are kept in a warm spot or brought indoors over winter, they can survive over several years. Collect the seeds at the end of the season for new pots the following year.

Verbena bonariensis – On a multitude of thin stems come hundreds of purple flowers that look splendid throughout the summer. Mixed with natural grasses, they make for a very modern border. Just one or two plants will go a long way to provide a real showstopper. Like *Perovskia*, leave the stems over winter for architectural interest and cut back at the start of spring, but beware – it is a prolific self-seeder.

Annuals

Ammi majus – A favourite of florists, and looking a little like a dainty version of cow parsley, this annual produces tall sprigs with a lacework of white flowers floating upon delicate green stems. A favourite too of birds and bees – leave the seeds on stems at the end of summer and they will provide nourishment for goldfinches that choose to overwinter in your garden.

Antirrhinum (snapdragons) – So named because their unusual flower shape looks a little like a dragon's mouth, *Antirrhinum* come in a huge range of colours, both bubblegum bright and candyfloss pastel. Easily grown from seed, once established in the garden they are great self-seeders, finding themselves nooks and crannies in which to make their home and flowering across the summer.

Calendula (marigold) – Planted near tomatoes, potatoes, squash and peppers, marigolds are said to have an aroma that drives away beetles, aphids and even rabbits. Perhaps slightly old-fashioned looking, their little yellow and orange heads dotted about the vegetable patch are very charming. They are easy to grow from seed each year and are prolific bloomers once established, bringing pops of colour to the vegetable garden.

Cosmos – A cottage garden stalwart. Easy as pie to grow from seed, whether in a pot or in a bed, they will need thinning as the seedlings grow. Just a few plants will fill a bed perfectly well with their wavering stems that offer a host of fairy-tale pink and white flowers. After flowering, let them go to seed and delay cutting them back – the next spring you will find little cosmos plants sprouting up where they have self-seeded. All you need to do is thin the seedlings and the next year's flower display for that bed is already prepared.

Lathyrus odoratus (sweet pea) – If planted early in the year, preferably started off indoors, nothing can compare to a romantic tower of tangled sweet peas across the summer. Coming in a host of colours, the sweet pea plants will need to be loosely tied into a wigwam or line of canes as they grow to give the tall stems support.

Nigella (love in a mist) – A slightly untidy affair, love in a mist is a low bush with romantic-looking blue flowers on a mess of spiky fronds. They are much loved by bees and look attractive dotted about the border in an apparently haphazard fashion – great for filling bare patches in a bed and easily sown from seed. Collect the black seeds from the brown seed pods, ready for sowing the following spring.

Papaver nudicaule (Icelandic poppy) – Sow these charming self-seeders one year and their delicate little blooms of orange, yellow and white will be popping up all over the place in the years to come. They thrive best in a sunny location and a well-drained soil, and will benefit from regular deadheading (cutting off the faded flowers).

Pelargonium – Marketed as 'geraniums' due to a botanical hangover, and often called a 'half-hardy geranium', these flowers are the backbone of a flower-filled summer patio. They look very cheery in terracotta or ceramic pots, and as summer goes on, they just keep giving, their fat red-orange flowers glowing vibrantly. Although officially an annual, they can last more than a year, but being half-hardy, they should come indoors for the winter to stand a chance of surviving.

Tropaeolum (nasturtium) – Once established, a tangle of nasturtium with their distinctive round yellow-green leaves and orange-yellow flowers is essential in any kitchen garden, attracting pests away from brassicas and legumes and providing a summer-long burst of colour. Very easy to grow from seed each spring. Although the orange-yellow is the classic, there are also varieties with blood red flowers and dark green leaves which are very striking.

Bulbs, Rhizomes & Corms

Allium – These are real attention-grabbers with their distinctive purple or white flowers that rest on a single stem, looking like a bursting firework. Coming in a range of sizes, some quite huge, they add pops of colour to a green border or one made up of grasses, and will look after themselves perfectly well, flowering from one year to the next. At the end of the season, leave the stalks to die back naturally which will feed the bulb and ensure a good display the following year. The dying leaves are a little ugly, but the dried flower heads have a majesty of their own.

Crocosmia – A mid- to late summer-flowering corm with thin stems bearing vibrant red or orange flowers amid lush green leaves. They are happy in a little shade, although they prefer the sun, and will grow well in most soils. Left to their own devices they will flower and die away each year, gently spreading

Crocus – These are late winter- and early spring-flowering, so the little purple and yellow heads of crocus appearing out of the grass beneath a tree are a delightful sign of spring. They fare well in sandy soil or in a stone trough set aside for them, but some specialist varieties are better suited to a dry and cool greenhouse.

SPRING FLOWERING BULBS

Snowdrops · Species Crocus · Crocus · Muscari · Hyacinth · Species Narcissus · Miniature Tulips · Tulips · Daffodils · Dutch Iris · Alliums

80cm · 40cm · 20cm · 10cm

Flowers FEBRUARY/MARCH   Flowers MARCH/APRIL   Flowers MARCH/MAY   Flowers MARCH/APRIL   Flowers MAY/JUNE

Cedric Morris 'Easter Bouquet'

Please take prepared bags only

BURFORD GARDEN CENTRE

Narcissus (daffodil) – Once planted in late summer these bulbs give joy for many years to come, entirely looking after themselves. The shoots grow out of the ground in spring and provide a host of yellow or yellow-white flowers. After the flowers have faded, like with allium, let the stems die back at their own pace, ready to flower again the following year.

Paeonia (peony) – Eternally romantic, like roses peonies come in all shades of pink, red, yellow and peach. There are two main types: the tree peony, which grows as a medium-sized bush, and the herbaceous peony, which lies dormant underground each winter before growing in mid-spring to form a small flowering bush. This type will need a ring-shaped support to stop the flowers falling under their own weight when they arrive in a short but splendid mid-summer display.

Tulipa (tulips) – Another spring-flowering bulb that offers blooms in every colour you can imagine. A little more formal than the *Narcissus*, for the best effect they should be planted in odd numbers in groups of at least seven in a sunny spot, although they can cope with a little shade. They look stunning in a large coloured pot, particularly one that contrasts with the colour of the flowers.

EASY VEGETABLES TO START WITH

There are many vegetables that are easy to grow direct from seed, and if you choose pest-resistant varieties, they don't take too much management before providing produce. The most productive plants are those that have a healthy start and water – but not too much. Allowing the soil to dry out a little sometimes actually encourages growth. Keep the bed and the area around it free of weeds and other vegetation to prevent overcrowding and reduce the risk of disease, and be sure to provide cane support for taller plants.

Easy vegetables to start with include: potatoes, tomatoes, spring onions, lettuce, spinach, pak choi, chard, dwarf beans, runner beans, peas, mangetout, edamame, cabbage, pumpkin and squash. Courgettes are usually a sure-fire hit, with just one plant providing abundant supply throughout the long season.

Aubergines, peppers and chillis can be grown in cooler climates with the aid of a cloche to raise the temperature around them, but thrive better in warmer climates or in a greenhouse.

TOMATO PLANT

BUTTERNUT SQUASH

Herbs can be dotted anywhere, and many – such as thyme – also act as companion plants, deterring pests with their aroma. If it's hot, be sure to water coriander and parsley well or they will 'bolt', growing tall and leggy and turning to seed. Basil sends a wonderful aroma throughout the vegetable patch, particularly a round ball of the piccolino dwarf basil, so it is always a good addition.

PUMPKIN

Tomatoes come in two types. One, called 'determinate', is a low bushy variety that won't need staking, and the other, called 'indeterminate', will need to be tied to a cane or stake as it grows. As soon as the indeterminate tomato plant starts flowering, pinch out the little shoots that grow between the main stem and its side branches. That way it will throw all its energy into a few main branches, creating a better crop of fruit and preventing the plant from becoming compacted and heavy.

HELPFUL TERMS

Annuals – Plants which flower in the same year the seed is planted, then set seed before dying away.

Bedding plants – Annuals and biennials used in the flower border.

Biennials – Plants which flower and set seed the year after their seed was planted, before dying away.

Bulbs, rhizomes, corms and tubers – These plants store their nutrients within a bulb, rhizome, corm or tuber planted underground. From it, green shoots grow and rise above the ground each year, then flower and die back to nothing again. Meanwhile, the roots grow down into the soil. Bulbs are spherical and include daffodils, tulips and onions. Rhizomes are generally flatter and longer, and include peonies and irises. Tubers are easily recognised in potatoes, but also include dahlias and begonias. Crocuses are corms.

Compost – Organic matter which is added to the soil to improve drainage and provide nutrients for growing plants.

Crop rotation – Rotating the position of three groups of vegetable crops (legumes, brassicas and root vegetables) so that they are never grown in the same place two years running.

Half-hardy – A plant that will tolerate frost, but which would not survive if left outside in a cold winter.

LILIES

48

FLOWER BULBS

Hardening off – Gently accustoming a young plant raised indoors from seed to the cooler temperatures outdoors.

Hardy – A plant that should survive over winter.

Herbaceous perennials – Plants that do not have a woody stem; these form the backbone of the flower garden, flowering and then dying back ready to grow and flower again the next year.

Hoeing – Using a hoe to lift or slice weeds from a vegetable or flower bed.

Mulch – A layer of organic matter (such as compost, leaf mould, bark or comfrey) or other insulating items such as wool or cardboard. Used to protect a plant from frost and inclement weather, and to allow nutrients to gently soak into the soil.

Perennial – A plant that grows every year and survives for more than two years.

Pricking out/thinning – In a seed tray or bed crowded with growing seedlings, retaining the strongest and removing others growing around them to be either discarded or planted elsewhere. Best done when the seedlings have a couple of pairs of leaves.

Self-seeders – Plants like cosmos and other flowering annuals that will drop seed and grow a new plant from the seed. When it's a plant you love, it's a blessing that it spreads naturally through the garden. But when it's a weed you don't want, it can be hell.

Let's Get Planting!

GROWING FROM SEED

There are many gorgeous flowers that are easy to grow from seed, including annuals (which will grow and bloom in a year before setting seed and then dying away), biennials (which will grow and then bloom in their second year before setting seed and dying away) and even some perennials (which will develop into plants that flower for several years).

Most of what gets planted in the vegetable patch is grown from seed afresh each year – beans, carrots, onions, lettuce, spinach, tomatoes and some herbs. They are all surprisingly easy to grow.

Some seeds must be grown indoors, while others must be sown directly outdoors. The back of the seed packet will give directions. When starting outdoors, sowing seeds early and then sowing more every two or three weeks, after the initial planting, allows the gardener to harvest throughout the season. This style of succession planting is great for carrots, spring onions, beans, beetroot, peas and squash.

When growing indoors, seeds can be started on a sunny windowsill or in a greenhouse and then planted out as seedlings or young plants. This allows the plant to mature earlier in the season, providing fruit or flowers for longer or earlier than would be the case otherwise.

Some seed packets will instruct you that the seed tray or pot should be placed in a propagator or covered with plastic to create the humidity needed for germination. For the plastic-free gardener, a sheet of glass from an old picture frame placed over the seed trays or pots will do the job.

When you sow indoors, be sure to acclimatise the young plants that grow from your seedlings to the cooler weather outside before planting them in a bed. Otherwise, they can wilt and die from the shock. If you have a cold frame – a mini greenhouse with a door that can be opened in the day and then closed again at night – it can be used for a week or so to get the young plant used to cooler temperatures. If you don't have access to a cold frame, you can still harden your plants off by bringing them outside each morning and then fetching them back indoors in the evening, acclimatising them gently in that way before planting out.

The plastic-free gardener has lots of options for what to grow seeds in, but the best solution will depend on what you are growing and whether you are planting in a shed or greenhouse where it doesn't matter if things are a little messy, or growing on a windowsill or table indoors.

Indoors, where you might have limited space, bamboo and metal trays are a great solution both for holding growing seedlings and as a base for holding DIY tubes and coir pellets. The trays are sturdy and waterproof, and can be used for many years over. But in a greenhouse, if there are lots of seeds to be planted, wood pulp modular trays and fibre pots are a cheap, easy solution – though they do tend to be wet to handle.

For the gardener who loves nothing better than to be messing about in the greenhouse or shed, soil blocking is a handy way of creating little chunks of growing material for seeds. There is an initial investment in the soil blocker, but after that no cost of pots at all – the only ongoing cost is the time and patience needed to make the blocks.

Before the growing season starts, check the back of your seed packets to see whether you need to sow the seeds early indoors and plant them out as seedlings, or if you can sow the seeds directly outdoors in the bed in which they will grow. Some plants might also prefer to be sown outdoors slightly later in the season, when the soil has warmed up sufficiently, so you may need to take that into account. The seed packets will provide directions and timings to help your plants thrive.

SEED TRAYS

Great for:
Peppers, chilli peppers, strawberries, aubergines, broccoli, artichoke, marigolds, pelargonium, Iceland poppy

You can use seed trays to start off any plant from seed, but they are most useful for tiny seeds that come many to a packet, and which germinate into seedlings that can be gently teased apart (always hold them by the new leaf when doing this, not by the stem).

To sow in a seed tray, fill it with potting compost, and water the compost before you sow the seeds. Sprinkle or carefully place the seeds on top, and then cover with a light layer of compost to the depth given in the seed packet instructions. To give the seeds an easier path, you can use a sieve to ensure the top layer of potting compost is of fine grade, but it's not essential. Some seeds should be planted to a depth of four or five centimetres, while others need just a sprinkle of soil above or will prefer to sit on the surface of the soil to germinate. The seed packet will give directions for what best suits the plant and variety you are working with. There are some seeds that will need soaking before sowing, so it is always a good idea to take a careful look at the packet and work out the seeds' requirements before you intend to sow them.

Keep the soil moist but not too wet, and place on a sunny windowsill or in a greenhouse.

After the seeds have germinated, the young seedlings will need 'pricking out' to thin them, leaving only the strongest seedlings and allowing them room to develop. If you are careful (always lifting the weaker seeds by a new leaf), they can be repotted on, doubling the number of seed trays planted up. The repotted seeds tend to grow into small, weaker plants at first, but so long as they are carefully watered, particularly when first repotted, they catch up over time. By the end of the season, it can often be difficult to tell the two sets of plants apart.

Pricking out sounds complicated, but it's a fairly practical matter and seedlings can be surprisingly robust so long as the stems are not touched. If a clump of seedlings is tangled, gently lift the whole clump out and pour a little water onto the soil bundle to naturally separate them.

Once they are large enough, you can transplant them into the ground or outdoor pot where they are to grow. If there is still danger of frost, transplant them into a larger pot indoors while waiting for the right conditions. If the young plant grows too big for its pot, its roots will start to circle the edges inside, harming its ability to become established when planted out, as it will be pot-bound.

Before planting them out, spend some time hardening off the seedlings by acclimatising them to outdoor temperatures.

Seed trays made of bamboo, wood and metal are all great and long-lasting alternatives to plastic.

Bamboo seed trays are available in most garden centres these days, and although an investment, they are attractive, easy to wipe clean and totally waterproof – a great solution for growing seedlings on a windowsill or table indoors. They will last several seasons and should then be compostable. Be sure to look for bamboo products that state they are 100% compostable. The EU recently banned some products being marketed as 'bamboo' (including some 'to-go' cups) which were in reality made from plastic with bamboo fibres added.

Metal trays do work for growing seeds, but results can be patchy, particularly if the tray is small. This is because there will be differences between the temperature of the soil close to the metal edge and in the centre of the tray. But for households that end up with lots of foil takeaway containers, they are a really economical solution for growing seeds, particularly if they would otherwise go in the recycling bin anyway. Just be sure to keep turning the trays and be prepared to pot on seedlings at different times as they develop at different rates.

Wooden trays have a great vintage look, but are not totally waterproof so are better used in a greenhouse or shed than on a windowsill in the house. They are also not as versatile as metal and bamboo trays, which can be used to grow seeds but also to house individual pots made from fibre or card and coir pellets.

WOODEN SEED TRAYS

MODULAR SEED TRAYS

Great for:
Peppers, chilli peppers, cabbage, most lettuce, radish, beetroot, oriental leaf, squash, nasturtium, pelargonium

Modular seed trays work well when it is beneficial to grow a little 'plug' of each seedling to be planted out with regimented spacing. They are perfect for more delicate plants, allowing the seedlings to be transplanted into bigger pots or directly outdoors without handling or damaging their roots.

For a gardener with lots of seeds to germinate, they are easier to work with than a multitude of small pots. They can also be used to double sowing capacity. Where seeds are grown at different times in pots and trays, the seedlings from a modular tray can be transferred into a batch of small pots just as the young plants they held have been removed and planted into the ground.

To prepare, fill the pockets of the modular seed tray with potting compost, and water the compost before adding the seeds. Cover them with a layer of potting compost to the depth instructed on the seed packet. Place on a sunny windowsill or in a greenhouse. Planting a couple of seeds in one pot is sometimes recommended (check the guidance on the back of the seed packet) as a form of insurance. The weaker seed is removed and discarded or potted into its own compartment if robust enough. Spend some time hardening off the seedlings once grown by acclimatising them to outdoor temperatures before planting them out.

Plastic-free options include modular seed trays made of coconut coir, wood pulp fibre and rubber. For those growing on a windowsill, a metal tray to keep the modular trays on is essential, especially for those made of coir or fibre, which will become damp.

Rubber modular trays are long-lasting, but require a greater initial up front investment. After use, be sure to wash and dry them thoroughly so that fungal disease does not grow inside, which would affect future seedlings' health. Wood pulp fibre trays are cheap and great for those in the greenhouse growing large numbers of seedlings, but will need to be purchased fresh each time, as they will become soggy and may already be decomposing by the time you come to plant out.

Be careful when sourcing coir and fibre modular trays online, as they can be shipped in heaps of unrecyclable plastic.

MODULAR SEED TRAYS

TUBE TRAINERS

Great for:
Plants that benefit from a long, strong root system, specifically legumes (broad beans, runner beans, French beans, peas and edamame), sweet peas and sunflowers; but also carrots, leeks and sweetcorn if you are not planting these directly into the ground

HOMEMADE TUBE TRAINERS

Like modular seed trays, tube trainers are designed to have one seed per compartment, but they are deeper than regular seed trays. The idea is that roots will be 'trained' to grow downwards and form a long, strong root network.

The length of the tube means that the roots of neighbouring seedlings don't join at the bottom of a tray and become tangled together, which would make it harder to separate the plants' roots without damaging them when potting on or planting out.

As the roots reach the bottom of the tube, the theory is they become 'air pruned', i.e., they stop growing. This encourages new roots to start to grow, creating a strong, complex root structure, particularly good for legumes.

To prepare each seed tube, place a palm over the bottom and fill the tube with potting compost. Slide it onto a waterproof tray, using a block to keep each tube upright as you add more until the tray is full. Water the compost from the top and from below by pouring water into the tray. When the compost is damp through, gently pour off any excess water, leaving just a small layer at the bottom of the tray which will continue to gently seep through. Put each seed into the centre of a tube, pushing it a little in or sprinkling potting compost on top until it is at the desired depth for germinating according to the seed packet's instructions.

Place the tray of tubes on a sunny windowsill or in a greenhouse. When ready for planting out, harden them off for a few days to first acclimatise the young plants to outdoor temperature.

The market for long seed-growing containers is heavily dominated by branded plastic products made of a brittle black and transparent plastic. Over time these crack and need to be discarded. But the good news is there are lots of alternatives. One in particular doesn't cost anything and its use for this purpose has grown in popularity over the last few years: the inner cardboard tubes of toilet rolls! These can only be used once, and will get soggy, so when growing new seedlings on a windowsill, be sure to use a metal or bamboo tray to hold the tubes in. An old cake tin does the job very well, so long as it is waterproof.

Once ready for planting out, tube trainers made of toilet roll inners can be planted straight into the ground. The cardboard will naturally disintegrate, if it hasn't started to already.

If you don't have access to enough toilet roll inners, you can purchase biodegradable fibre tubes. They are more robust than cardboard rolls and don't get as soggy or disintegrate as quickly. They are designed to be planted into the ground along with the young plant, where they will decompose to nothing as the plant grows.

There are also rubber tube trainers which, like modular seed trays, can be used many times over but will involve a bigger upfront investment. These are made of organic wood, paper pulp and bitumen. They must be washed and dried well after use to prevent the growth of fungi which would harm later seedlings' progress.

Place the tray of tubes on a sunny windowsill or in a greenhouse and water them from the bottom up if possible.

Despite all best efforts, when you have a number of long fibre or compostable pots close together, it is hard to prevent little mushrooms sometimes growing from the soil, but they are easily pinched or knocked off.

SMALL POTS

Great for:
Peppers, tomatoes, aubergines, herbs, squash, sweetcorn, courgettes, pumpkins, melons, strawberries, cosmos, nasturtium, pelargonium, lavender

Small pots are great for larger seeds that can be easily handled, and for plants that will be planted out singly – you can do this either by transferring them first to a larger pot, or by directly planting them out where they are to grow to a mature plant.

Fill the pot with potting compost, and water it well. Place the seed in the centre and cover it with a layer of potting compost to the depth specified by the seed packet. Sometimes the instructions might guide you to put two seeds in the pot together. When the seeds germinate, gently tease out the weaker seedling which can be discarded or potted up into another pot.

Place the pot on a sunny windowsill or in a greenhouse and keep the soil damp but not soggy. When the young plants are ready to be planted out, be sure to spend some days hardening them off, so that they become accustomed to outdoor temperatures.

There are lots of different types of pots on the market that you can use for sowing seeds, and also some kinds, such as newspaper pots, that you can make yourself. Of those available to purchase, there are single-use pots made of fibre which are cheap and easy to use, or multi-use ones made of bamboo, husk and coir.

There are pros and cons to different pots. Some fibre pots tend to get soft as the seedlings and the young plants they grow into are watered, and will tear easily if not handled carefully, but are the cheapest to buy and therefore the most economical if there is a lot of planting to be done. There are more expensive but more robust fibre ones on the market too, which hold moisture in the pot better – in my experience, supporting a healthy young plant.

When considering which pots are best for your use, you should factor in convenience, how tidy you need to be in your growing space, budget and how many seeds you will be sowing. The pros and cons of all the different options are considered a few pages over.

FIBRE POTS

SOIL BLOCKERS

The first of two entirely pot-free solutions to germinating seeds and growing young plants, soil blocking is a method of creating tubes of soil in which seedlings can grow. It works on the principle of compressing soil into blocks that are firm enough to hold together as a growing medium without a pot. Use the smaller blocks in place of modular trays and the larger blocks in place of small pots.

The type of potting compost used is extremely important, as the blocks need enough grit or vermiculite in the potting compost to ensure they are not too dense when compressed, yet not so much that they cannot hold a firm structure. Water must be able to soak through the compressed block and roots should be able to grow through it without too much resistance.

As the tips of the roots reach the edges of the block they are 'air-pruned' and stop growing, triggering the growth of new roots, which helps ensure a healthy root system and also prevents the plant becoming root-bound. This is when the roots form a compacted tangle, chasing each other in circles around the pot, which restricts the young plant's development when it is planted out.

Buying the soil blocker kit is something of an investment, and kits do contain plastic parts within the tool, but once purchased, if they work for you, they could replace the annual cost of buying modular fibre seed trays and small pots for starting seeds off.

They are a little 'hands on' to use, so not the best for those potting up seeds in the house to grow on a windowsill, and the smallest tools can be fiddly for some.

Some retailers sell the soil blockers singly or in kits with all the necessary equipment, offering different size block makers.

For soil blocking, you'll also need one or more metal or bamboo trays to keep the blocks on. That way you can water them gently from below without risking the blocks becoming unstable or disintegrating.

SOIL BLOCKS

COIR PELLETS

An alternative to soil blocking, coir pellets (or discs) are small cylinders of coir and compost that have been pre-sealed into tubular slices ready for seed germination. Use them in place of modular seed trays.

The compressed pellets will expand when watered and some come with a small fibre pot to hold the expanded compost. Some have an indent for the seed; others do not.

Their main advantage is that they can easily be purchased without any plastic or plastic packaging being involved, and they avoid the need to source potting compost in plastic-free packaging if you are not making your own.

As with peat moss, the basic coco coir does not contain the nutrients plants need to support their growth, so its raw material must be mixed with compost or fertiliser to be a complete replacement to peat-based compost.

The coir pellets are ready mixed and easy to use. They don't come with the mess of soil blocking and, when combined with a waterproof tray made of metal or bamboo, they offer a great option for those growing seeds indoors on windowsills or in the greenhouse. However, they will require purchasing each time as they are single-use items, whereas the soil blocker, once bought, has no cost if you have potting compost.

Another advantage of the pellets is that, as with the soil blocks, the tips of the roots are air-dried as they reach the edges of the pellets, encouraging the growth of new roots and so promoting a strong root network. As with soil-block grown plants stand-alone coir pellets prevent the root-bound issues that you can get with hard pots, so they are a great way to start off healthy young plants.

The disadvantage of coir pellets is that you can't choose the exact type of compost in which you will grow your seedlings, in the same way that you could if growing in cardboard, fibre or rubber pots, tubes or soil blocking. And the pellets do need a close eye on them on a regular basis to make sure they don't dry out.

As with soil blocks, you'll also need one or more metal or bamboo trays to keep the pellets on. The tray(s) will make watering from below easier so that the pellets do not crumble if not in fibre pots, and so that the seeds are not displaced.

COIR PELLETS GROWN IN FIBRE POTS

LET'S TALK ABOUT COIR

Made of the fibres found between the hard shell of a coconut and its hairy outer coat, coir has been used since ancient times to produce rope and cord, and in the nineteenth century it began to be exported around the world for the manufacture of carpets, matting, sacking and furniture upholstery.

A natural, totally renewable product, coir is increasingly being used as a substitute for plastic in the shape of moulded plant pots. The majority of the world's coir fibre comes from India and Sri Lanka, though it is also extensively produced in Thailand and Vietnam.

Coir pots for horticultural use are moulded, often by hand, and then shipped by boat around the world. A sustainable, environmentally friendly solution to plastic pots, they naturally biodegrade over time and can be planted directly into the soil along with the plant, or can be stripped away and composted.

Coconut coir also forms the basis for a potting compost called coir peat or coco peat, which is increasingly being used as a substitute for peat compost.

Historically, gardeners have used peat moss as a growing medium for seedlings

COIR COMPOST

and new plants. Harvested from bogs in both the northern and southern hemispheres, peat moss is packaged up and shipped to garden centres and nurseries around the world. It derives from sphagnum, a moss that grows in wetlands and which naturally compacts over millennia into a rich peat, sterile and devoid of harmful weed seeds or bacteria. This, along with its fantastic water-retention properties, traditionally made peat moss the perfect growing material.

But it is not a sustainable resource: there's a finite amount of it, and the digging up of peat bogs releases carbon dioxide into the atmosphere. This is believed to be a major contributor to global warming. As consciousness of this grows, the horti-cultural industry and growers alike are looking to alternatives to peat moss, and coco peat is one of the options.

Like peat moss it is sterile, has good water retention properties and doesn't compact in the way that soil does, allowing air to access roots. But, also like peat moss, it doesn't contain nutrients, so in the same way that peat moss is mixed with compost to create a growing medium, coco peat must be mixed with something like compost or fertiliser to provide nutrients to the growing plant.

You can buy coco peat or coco coir in the form of a dehydrated block, but these blocks always seem to come wrapped in plastic. So, for the plastic-free gardener, the best use of coco peat at the moment is in the form of coco pellets or discs, which are readily available in plastic-free packaging in 'ready-to-go' sets.

Lots of Pots

In 2018, a study by *Horticulture Week* found that around half a billion plastic plant pots were ending up in landfill or being incinerated in the UK each year.[17] Many of the pots in which plants were sold at the time were not recyclable, either because they were made of black plastic or an unrecyclable plastic polymer, or because local recycling processors couldn't handle the soil contamination.

Many gardeners have a collection of plastic plant pots that have accumulated over the years. It's pretty difficult to tell which are recyclable and which aren't. Most are made of high-density polyethylene (HDPE), low-density polyethylene (LDPE) or polystyrene (PS), and come in a variety of colours. None of these plastics are readily recyclable.

Since that shocking figure of half a billion plastic plant pots sent to landfill or incineration each year was publicised, there has been a concerted effort across nurseries and garden stores to offer plants in recyclable taupe pots, and local councils have improved their offering of pot recycling. However, even now, many of them still cannot go into household recycling collections but must instead be taken to specialist recycling centres, a chore which is likely to lead to a significant number of them ending up in landfill at the end of their useful life regardless.

And as discussed earlier, much of recycling is really only one cycle of 'downcycling'. PET pots are made into PET pellets, which are used to create clothes of synthetic fibres, which can't be recycled. Instead, they end up being sent to landfill or incinerated.

The great news is that, for the plastic-free gardener growing from seed, the choice of alternative plastic-free receptacles for starting off seeds in pots and for potting on is fantastic. In addition to coir, there is also moulded wood pulp, fabric, zinc, cardboard, bamboo, rubber, and even wool.

FIBRE POTS

Generally made from wood pulp, fibre pots are biodegradable and theoretically can be planted directly into the earth. Stiff, cheap and generally single use, the cheapest versions are a good option when you are growing large numbers of seeds and have lots of potting on to do. If you buy in bulk they are even better value for money, and can be found packaged in large card boxes.

There is a wide variety of sizes and two main types with slightly different price points: an economical version which is more porous, will deteriorate more quickly and will need vigilant watering; and a more robust but more expensive branded version.

Plants can be planted into their final position outdoors along with the pot to protect against shock. The fibre will eventually break down on its own over time, if it isn't starting to do so already when you come to plant out.

Be careful when sourcing fibre pots. When bought online, some are shipped internationally and come wrapped in heaps of non-recyclable plastic, but they are now widely offered in garden centres with card packaging.

The cheaper versions can get a little soggy with use, so be aware that you might want to place them on a waterproof tray when watering. If you are used to growing seedlings in plastic pots, then be aware that the growing seedlings in these pots will need watering on a more regular basis, because the porous nature of the pots means they dry out more quickly.

FIBRE POT

At planting out time, the fibre can be peeled away and discarded, placed on the compost heap or planted with the plant to slowly decompose.

Pros: Inexpensive, biodegradable, easy to handle

Cons: Can only be used once, cheaper versions dry out quickly if not watered vigilantly, must check the retailer does not package or ship them in plastic wrap

PAPER POTS

PAPER POTS

When you first start trying to garden plastic-free, one of the first gifts from family is often a paper pot maker. These little gadgets let you create lots of pots from leftover newspapers. So, if you have a household which takes a lot of newspapers that end up in the recycling bin, this is a great option.

There is a one-off investment in the purchase, but theoretically it's cost-free from then on for anyone with spare paper to use. The only drawback is that the pots are fiddly to make, so best suited to those who love whiling away the time in a green-fingered way, not for those in a hurry.

The pots made are a fixed variety of sizes. Like fibre and cardboard, they can only be used once, and will soon start to disintegrate. They are best used for quickly growing seedlings that will be planted out after not too long, and will need to be used with a seed tray to hold them – metal if you are indoors, or otherwise a wooden tray is fine for the greenhouse or potting shed.

The paper pot can be planted with the plant, but if you are concerned it is too thick and might delay the roots from developing, you can remove or loosen it. If you are doing this, it is better to loosen the paper slowly while hardening the young plant off.

Pros: After the initial investment, a really cheap way of producing lots of little pots

Cons: Can get a bit messy, fiddly to make, each pot only suitable for short growing durations

HEMP POTS

Hemp pots are a great alternative to the plastic tubs used to grow tomato and potato plants. Like their plastic counterparts, hemp pots are a boon for those with limited growing space or with a patio-focused garden. They come in a range of sizes, from around five to forty litres.

Made of hemp, and usually stitched with cotton thread, they derive from a sustainable source, and are fully biodegradable.

They can be reused for several seasons over, and when they wear out can be put on the compost. Water can seep out of the bottom during their use, so it is worth taking that into consideration when deciding on where to position them.

If you are used to using plastic tubs, hemp pots will be more porous, meaning the plants inside will tend to dry out quicker, so be vigilant with your watering.

Pros: Great for patio areas for growing on individual large plants to maturity

Cons: Will need to consider water seepage at base and water vigilantly in hot weather

BAMBOO AND HUSK POTS

Bamboo pots can be very attractive and are great for growing on indoors, in a mini greenhouse or on a patio. They come in different colours, with a modern aesthetic. Durable and able to hold their shape as well as plastic, they can be used many times over and won't get soggy.

Usually made from bamboo and rice, and held together with a naturally occurring resin, they will eventually biodegrade and can go on the compost heap. However, be careful when sourcing, to ensure that the product doesn't contain plastic as well as bamboo fibres. Make sure the pots' packaging say they are 100% compostable.

Bamboo pots are great for plants that you want to keep in the pot for a few months, and ideal for propagating hardwood cuttings. They are more expensive than coir and fibre pots, so not ideal if you are growing lots of seedlings at once. But they are attractive, and can be used many times over.

Similar looking and handled in the same way, pots made from the husk of vegetable crops, including coconut and grain, can also be used a few times and are biodegradable so can be composted when worn out.

Pros: Longer lasting, pretty for a modern look, eventually biodegradable, easy to handle without too much mess

Cons: More expensive than the single-use options

BURFORD GARDEN CENTRE

COIR POTS

Made from the outer fibres of coconuts, coir pots are a great alternative to plastic. Light, durable and able to hold their shape well, they are inexpensive to buy in bulk. For those nurseries selling plants with a plastic-free or plastic-free delivery promise, they are starting to become a common alternative to plastic pots.

You can buy the pots in bulk online, and many garden centres are now starting to stock them too. Just be sure to check the retailer can provide them in plastic-free packaging. Given that they are a product designed to be a replacement for plastic, you'd be surprised how many retailers package them up and ship them out in plastic packaging which isn't even recyclable.

The coir pots are great for plants which you might have grown in the greenhouse, and which need potting on to a large pot and then hardening off.

When the plants are ready to go in the ground, you can gently remove the pot and reuse it. When they become too tatty, collect several and use them as a mulch in the winter or early spring. You can plant the pot and plant together, but I have found that it's better to peel the pot away. Otherwise on hot days, water in the surrounding soil doesn't easily make its way through the coir barrier, which takes a long time to biodegrade, and you need to be vigilant about watering inside the rim of the planted pot.

One caveat – be careful not to leave plants in the sun without water if you are not ready to plant them for a few days. Plants in coir pots will dry out quicker than those in plastic, which is less permeable.

COIR POT

Eventually the pots can go on the compost, but they take a long time to biodegrade, so using the coir as a mulching material might serve your garden better.

Pros: Inexpensive, biodegradable, easy to handle, with care can be reused a few times over

Cons: Will need replaced after a few uses, can dry out quickly while waiting to plant out if you are not able to water on a regular basis, must check the retailer does not package and ship them in plastic wrap

WOOL POTS

Made from raw washed wool, these cute little pots are a very attractive natural alternative to plastic. They can be used to start seedlings, but they also make a perfect receptacle for decorative plants that will sit in a prominent position while they are growing larger – a great talking point for plastic-free gardening.

They need to be stood in a waterproof tray or dish so that they can be watered bottom-up, which will encourage strong downward root growth and prevent the wool from becoming discoloured at the top.

BURFORD GARDEN CENTRE

Once planted out, the wool pot can be removed and arranged around the plant to deter slugs and snails.

Pros: Attractive, simple to use, in some cases locally produced

Cons: More expensive than other single-use pots

TERRACOTTA AND CERAMIC POTS

Though expensive, when it comes to plant pots, there is not much that compares to the rustic charm of terracotta pots. Literally meaning 'baked earth', terracotta is a ceramic made from the firing of clay. It is often associated with Italy, but terracotta is also used extensively in artworks and ceramics across China and India.

Terracotta pots are durable and, if collected steadily over the years, become the backbone of any working garden, offering a ready pot for a month or two of growing on; a permanent home for repeat-flowering half-hardy perennials such as bright orange pelargonium; or a decorative feature for a greenhouse or shed when arranged in lopsided piles, particularly those with pretty scalloped edges.

As they grow in size, the price tag of terracotta pots starts to become prohibitive, and most larger ceramic pots for permanent or seasonal decorative plants are made of clay fired at a higher temperature. When purchasing a ceramic pot, it's worthwhile paying a little extra to obtain one marked 'frost-proof'. 'Frost-resistant' will not last as long, and those with no mark at all might seem like a good bargain, but with one cold winter they start to fall to pieces.

TERRACOTTA POTS

Pros: Extremely attractive, protect plants both from the cold and the heat very well, will last many seasons (and perhaps, if handled carefully, many generations)

Cons: More expensive and heavier than other options, will break if knocked or dropped

METAL POTS

Metal pots look attractive, particularly when arranged along a windowsill, and they can often be found for sale in kits designed for that very purpose. They are usually made of zinc. You can also pick up interesting ones at vintage shops, for a mix-and-match feel.

They are not the ideal container for growing on small plants, as the metal can become hot when exposed to direct heat or sun in a way that terracotta pots don't, but when placed on a windowsill where the plants will not get scorched, they can provide a smart interior aesthetic.

Pros: Attractive indoors for small numbers of plants

Cons: Not the perfect growing container

SEED MARKERS

Whichever solution or mix of solutions you choose for germinating seeds and growing young plants, if you are planning to work with lots of pots or a large selection of different seeds, then seed markers are essential – otherwise it's remarkably easy to be stumped a few days later as to what a newly growing plant might be.

The cheapest and easiest to use are wooden sticks that look like lollipops. Be careful when sourcing these, as many options available come in plastic packaging. Some ink will fade on them quickly, so experiment for a more permanent label. Bamboo and slate markers are also very attractive, and can be reused, but tend to be more expensive.

WOODEN SEED MARKERS

Planting Out

Once seedlings have grown into small plants, they are ready to be planted out into patio planters, or into their growing positions in the flower or vegetable beds. If you have a *potager*-style garden where flowers and vegetables mingle in a relaxed confusion, you could be planting them together.

Beds always benefit from some preparation. If you have time in the autumn before the planting season, dig them over and let the winter frosts break up the clods of earth. If you find they are chock-full of weeds, cut them down or hoe them out as much as you can, and then lay a mulch over the top of the earth that will exclude all light. Old carpet is the traditional favourite for the job,

but these days carpet often has a foam plastic backing which will disintegrate into the soil. Plastic-free alternatives are cardboard, which is readily available for free but will need to be replaced every month or so, or a biodegradable mulch mat. For smaller areas, there are mulch mats made of wool and coir, but I have found the latter can be difficult to purchase without plastic packaging, so a little care is needed when sourcing. Effectively suppressing the weeds in this way takes six months and you may find some persistent ones will survive.

If you are new to your garden, it is worth trying to figure out whether your soil is clay-based or sandy. Take up a handful of it after rain. If it is gritty and crumbly, it's sandy. If it compresses into a texture that looks like something you might stick on a potter's wheel, and if you can't get it off the fork without the help of the edge of a boot, it's clay-based. There are kits you can buy to test it, which will be more accurate than the above method, and which will also tell you the pH or acidity of the soil, but these kits are plastic.

If you are a new gardener, plastic-free gardening is much easier if you work with plants that like your soil. That way you won't have to figure out how to alter it by sourcing lime, grit or specialist fertilisers in a plastic-free way. For ideas, take a walk around the neighbourhood and see what plants others have in their gardens. Plants that you see locally on a regular basis are probably a great fit for your garden too.

Most soils will benefit from the periodic addition of organic matter, such as compost leaf mould or well-rotted manure. If your soil is very heavy clay or thin sand, then the addition of a good growing compost to the hole in which you are planting will benefit your seedlings when they are planted out.

Always give a plant a really good soak before taking it out of the pot for planting, then water it regularly after planting and keep watering it, particularly if the weather is dry, until it becomes established.

If you find the roots of your plant have become tangled when you take it out of its pot, gently tug some of the roots free with your fingers and spread them out before planting the new plant. That way its roots will have the best chance of spreading and creating a strong root base for growth. Place the plant in a hole that is deeper and wider than its girth after the addition of compost, then fill the hole back in and gently firm the surface down. For trees and shrubs, most gardening experts advise not to add extra nutrients at the time of planting, so that the roots are encouraged to reach down and form a deep root structure.

If you are planting something into heavy clay that will grow tall and develop deep roots, dig the hole a bit deeper still, and put a layer of the broken-up clay into the hole before continuing as normal. This ensures the roots of the plant don't find themselves travelling through a lovely gentle compost mix only to suddenly hit heavy clay. If this happens, they tend to 'curl up their toes', as the saying goes, meaning they develop a shallow root base, creating a less stable plant or tree as a result.

MOVING A SELF-SEEDED COSMOS

HARDENING OFF

If you have been growing your seed-lings and young plants indoors or in a greenhouse, you will need to gently acclimatise them to cooler and less humid conditions before planting them in their permanent outdoor position. Wait until they have a few leaves, not counting the two little cotyledons or 'seed leaves' that first come out of the seed.

Hardening off can be done by placing the seedlings or young plants in a cold frame, opening it up to bring in the temperate daytime air and closing it again to keep the plant warm overnight, or by bringing them manually outside each day and back in again at night. After two or three weeks of this gentle introduction to the outside world, they will be ready to be transferred without suffering from shock, which can cause tender plants to wither and die.

VEGETABLE CROP ROTATION

For the vegetable garden, there are certain vegetables which ideally should not be planted in the same location across two consecutive years. The relevant vege-tables are divided into three groups: brassicas (broccoli, cauliflower and cabbage); legumes (peas and beans); and

root vegetables (potatoes, parsnips, onions, leeks, turnips and beetroot). Each group is grown in a different section of your garden, and then their planting position is rotated the following year to a new slot.

This rotation ensures pests that target each particular set of plants do not have a chance to build up a presence in a bed over successive years, but instead are starved of their prey. Some of the groups also add nutrients to the soil which benefit other groups. For example, legumes provide nitrogen to the soil, which helps support the growth of brassicas the following year.

So when figuring out where to put your vegetables, if you are growing from all the different groups, it is worth separating your beds into at least three distinct areas and keeping a record of what you have grown where.

Other types of vegetable and fruit, such as lettuce, oriental leaves, spinach, courgettes, tomatoes, strawberries, pumpkin and squash, can be grown in any of the beds.

Many vegetable seeds can be planted directly into the ground – such as carrot, spring onion, runner beans, dwarf beans, peas, lettuce, spinach and oriental leaves. When planting up a bed, it's a great idea to mark the line with a string held a little way off the ground by a cane at each end. Then, as you weed, you will easily be able to distinguish your new seedling from probable weeds.

Use natural twine, often made of jute, for this. An essential to have at hand, you can find it either in brown or dyed an array of colours. As well as for marking out planting lines, you can use it to create supports for beans and to tie taller plants such as tomatoes and sweet peas to stakes as they grow.

ANTIRRHINUM (SNAPDRAGONS)

FLOWER BEDS

If you are growing flowers from seed for a flower bed, it's worth taking a moment when choosing your seeds to think about which colours will work best together. You might be after a random riot of colour, but many gardeners work to a colour scheme.

A colour wheel is a great way to think about which colours complement each other. If you pick colours which are opposite each other on the wheel, the display created is vibrant and interesting. Purples and yellows are often planted together, for example. Or choose colours which are next to each other on the wheel and they will blend together in a harmonious and natural way.

Reds are best used sparingly as they will grab the eye in any bed, but they work brilliantly en masse on a sun-soaked wall, or where the evening sun will fall and catch them.

Another idea could be a bed focused on one particular colour, such as all white, which creates a focus on the form and structure of the flowers, standing out against the lush greenery. Or a romantic muddle of pinks, reds and whites can work well too.

To support biodiversity of insect, animal and birdlife, consider keeping sections of the garden wilder and sowing wildflowers. This can be just a corner or strip of the lawn or, if you have the space, a section laid over to a wildflower meadow.

Soil Improvers

Most beds benefit from the addition of organic materials, particularly where the natural detritus of garden leaves and decaying plant debris is tidied away and prevented from returning its nutrients to the soil. Plants need light, water and nutrients such as nitrogen, phosphate and potash to help them grow strong stems, flowers, fruit and roots.

Most fertilisers available on the market are in plastic containers, although there are some sold in cardboard packaging. Organic soil improvers provide nutrients to growing plants but also improve drainage for both sandy and clay soils.

To enhance the quality of soil in your flower or vegetable beds in a plastic-free way, you can make your own leaf mould, peat-free compost or comfrey feed.

LEAF MOULD

Creating leaf mould is as simple as it sounds. Just collect leaves that have fallen in the autumn into a pile in a shady part of your garden and allow them to rot down over a year or two. Add water occasionally if the weather is particularly hot and you see that the pile is drying out. You might want to keep the leaves in a metal enclosure to stop them blowing away when first gathered. In any event, be careful not to collect leaves where there are invasive weeds present, in case you spread them to other parts of your garden when you dig the leaf mould into a bed or use it as a mulch. You can include the needles of conifers, but they won't readily break down for at least two years, so are best left to rot on a separate pile. Leaf mould is generally slightly acidic, and that from pine needles is doubly so. Use leaf mould from pine needles to mulch or to dig into the soil for ericaceous (acid-loving) plants such as azaleas, camellias, hydrangeas, acers, blueberries and raspberries.

MAKING COMPOST

You can purchase compost from retailers, but it is difficult to do so at scale without involving plastic. Compost that comes in

plastic-free packaging tends to be offered in smaller quantities and can be expensive.

To make compost, it is useful to have two wooden bins or enclosures: one to house the compost heap you are currently building, and one full one which is either maturing or ready for use. It's best to site the compost heaps away from sitting areas – built with the right ingredients they shouldn't smell unpleasant, but they can have a strong earthy aroma. They are best placed in a shady or part-shaded spot, so that they stay moist and don't dry out.

Making compost is much easier than it sounds. Start with a base of chopped-up woody stems or branches that will allow air to circulate below the pile. Above that, add a layer of roughly 15 cm of each of the following: kitchen waste (eggshells, coffee grounds, plastic-free teabags, vegetable and fruit peelings); green waste (grass cuttings, leaves, old bedding plants and flowers); fibrous waste (brown cardboard, straw, shredded newspapers, fibrous stems).

Follow these three layers with a layer of soil or manure, around 2.5 cm deep. Repeat with the waste layers and soil layer, adding to them over time when you can, until the bin is full. It's best to set aside material so that you can add several

Once the pile is built, cover it and leave it for one to three months before turning it over. Many people cover their compost heap with tarpaulin or old carpet, but as these can be made of or backed with plastic, the plastic-free gardener can use brown cardboard instead. However, check the pile every now and again to ensure it is not getting too wet inside, which can make the compost slimy.

Turning the pile over with a fork adds air and swaps the material at the edges of the pile with that in the centre. Turn it for the first time sooner rather than later if it is compacted, slimy or too damp. After that, turn it every month or so. It will take between four and twelve months for the pile to decompose into a dark, crumbly compost ready for use.

layers at once, rather than adding them in bit by bit.

Try not to add meat, fish, cooked food or strong-smelling food to the compost, to avoid attracting vermin. Don't add dog poo, cat litter or nappies, and for plastic-free gardening, be especially careful not to add cardboard or paper which is laminated with plastic, giving it a shiny look. If you are not sure whether your teabags are plastic-free, avoid adding them. Many brands of teabags are still made with synthetic fibres, though fortunately those without are now becoming increasingly available. To ensure the pile does not attract flies, be sure not to leave it with the kitchen waste pile uppermost – always try to finish with a green waste or soil layer.

Dig your compost into beds in the autumn or winter to improve the quality of the soil, or use it to add nutrients to the soil when potting out plants.

Don't use this compost for potting new seeds. Homemade compost tends to be too rich for this purpose and will not have enough drainage. To make potting compost, blend two parts of the garden compost with one part leaf mould and add something to prevent the mixture from compacting and to ensure good drainage, such as vermiculite, perlite, grit, sand or shells for drainage. If the seedlings are going to be growing on to become small plants in the same pots, then add some topsoil into the mix too, to give it a bit more substance for when you plant out.

BUYING COMPOST

Buying compost, bark and well-rotted manure without plastic being involved in the process is pretty tricky.

In smaller quantities, it is possible to find specialist compost sold in biodegradable brown stand-up pouches. The bags don't become soggy and are resistant to water damage because they have a plastic-like inner lining made of a biodegradable 'polythene', created from plant-based starch. Where you don't have the space for a compost heap, this is a great alternative, but quantities tend to be small and although the quality can be high, so can the price point.

The other option, if planning to use a fair quantity, is to have organic material delivered in a bulk plastic container from a provider that will collect or receive the container back afterwards to reuse. There are also some smaller retailers who sell compost locally using a (plastic) reusable 'bag for life', and some garden

CRUSHED WHELK SHELLS AND PISTACHIO NUT SHELLS

centres are now starting to accept soil-contaminated polythene compost bags for specialist recycling.

It's best to buy compost labelled 'peat-free', as the destruction of the world's peat reserves to create peat compost is unsustainable and is believed to be a major contributor to global warming. But beware peat-free compost that appears to come in cardboard boxes – there can sometimes be a plastic container inside the box.

MAKING COMFREY FEED

Fertilisers will help provide additional nutrients to growing plants, promoting healthy and abundant fruit and flowers. To avoid buying feed products in plastic packaging, you can make your own organic version by growing comfrey and creating a nitrogen-rich liquid fertiliser from its leaves.

Like leaf compost, it is fairly simple to make, but needs a little forward planning. First, set aside an area to grow the comfrey in. The plant is harmful to eat and can be irritating to the skin and eye, so choose its growing position bearing that in mind; you might also want to wear gloves when harvesting it. It has a tendency to spread from its deep tap roots and can become invasive, so keep it to a contained area where you control its growth, and either grow a variety called 'Bocking 14' which is sterile and cannot self-seed, or be sure to cut it down before it flowers. If using Bocking 14, you can still propagate it by digging up a plant and potting up chunks of the root in sections.

To make the feed, sow the comfrey from seed and when mature, cut down the plant, strip the leaves and place them in a large bucket. (The stems can go on the compost pile.) Compress the leaves, adding as many as you can, and weigh them down with a brick or large rock. Add water and cover the bucket – as the brewing mixture does not smell pleasant – and leave it for around three weeks. When it has turned into a thick, dark liquid, it is ready to be diluted. Use one part comfrey liquid to ten parts water, or dilute further for young plants. Store the feed in a watering can kept aside for the purpose and apply the liquid directly to the roots of fruit and flower-bearing plants. It is a fabulous feed for tomato and potato plants, as well as for aubergine and peppers. It can be applied directly to the base of the plant, or alternatively it can be sprayed directly onto leaves.

Any leftover comfrey you have can be added to the compost heap to boost the nitrogen content of your compost, and any spare leaves can also be added to plants as a mulch around their base.

Protecting Your Plants

PROTECTING FROM FROST

If you want to plant out fruit and vegetable plants early in the growing season or extend the season to winter crops, it will be essential to protect your more tender plants from exposure to frost with a cloche or tunnel. Early in the season the cloches and tunnels are used to warm up the soil prior to planting, and throughout the growing season they can also be used to create a microclimate, for any plant which needs a warmer environment than you have in your region. For example, glass dome cloches are great for starting off chilli peppers and sweet peppers.

Because plastic dome cloches and synthetic fleece tunnels are cheap and relatively robust, over the last couple of decades they have been the primary type manufactured. However, it is still possible to source glass ones – either newly made or in vintage gardening shops. They are significantly more expensive, but if handled carefully will last a long time.

There are two types. Less expensive are the French bell jars – these are glass domes that sit over a single plant. The other type is the Victorian style of cloche, rather like a mini square greenhouse made of glass on a cast-iron frame. Though expensive, they are long-lasting and add a definite grandeur to the vegetable bed. If you do choose to go for this option, shop around as there is huge variety in prices. There are antique and vintage ones available, but because they are such collectable items, they are often at least as expensive as newly made ones.

Both bell jar and Victorian-style cloches will need to be sourced carefully for the plastic-free garden, because if ordered online, they can come with one of our 'uglies': unrecyclable polystyrene packaging bricks.

GLASS CLOCHES

Fleeces play a similar role to cloches, keeping plants protected from frosts, but are easier to use to warm long strips of plants or lines of early grown seedlings. As with cloches, the market for fleece tunnels is dominated by products made of plastic.

I have not been able to find a bio-degradable alternative to soft fleece tunnels that is specifically made for lines of seedlings, but one option is making a DIY version from biodegradable netting to provide a little shelter.

As with most plastic-free solutions, planning ahead helps. When deciding where to plant your more tender plants, consider where your garden's hot and cold spots are. Anything exposed to a prevailing wind will be cooler. Spots sheltered by a hedge or fence will be warmer, and any beds up against a brick wall facing the sun will be much warmer – ideal for growing fruit.

Otherwise, the alternative and somewhat pragmatic solution is to run a shorter vegetable-growing season and keep growing on any seedlings in your greenhouse or on your windowsills until all risk of frost has passed. You can also grow on in pots which can be brought into a shed, garage or other warmer protected space if a frost is forecast for that night.

For trees and shrubs that need protecting over winter, look for inventive alternatives to plastic fleece – for example, you can use old clothing, sheets or newspapers stuffed with straw.

PROTECTING FROM PESTS

The interference of pests, whether of the small nibbling type or the buzzing-about type, can be heart-breaking to the fruit and vegetable gardener, even without the added complication of being plastic-free.

Much of the kitchen gardener's work seems to involve battling caterpillars, slugs, snails, rabbits, deer and bugs, not to mention naturally occurring moulds and fungi, which can take over all your planting of a particular fruit or vegetable.

Be prepared to lose some of your crop to these natural predators, however careful you are. But the good news is that while some may be lost, not all will be and over time you will find the things you can grow that don't succumb so easily. There are also several ways to make life harder for pests, before you even turn to physical barrier protections.

When sourcing seeds, look for pest-tolerant versions. For example, many carrot varieties are bred to be resistant to carrot root fly, and there are tomatoes bred to be resistant to blight. When preparing your planting beds, make sure the borders around them are clear of vegetation such as long grass or weeds, which make it easier for pests to transfer to the vegetables. Instead, create clear borders around your beds. A margin of rough ground, with a sprinkling of bark, gravel, pistachio shells or crushed seashells, for example, makes it harder for crawling insects to reach your produce.

At the start of the season, consider companion planting when figuring out what to plant where. Some companion plants work by giving off an aroma which is unpleasant to pests; others attract insects which prey on the pests; and some will attract the pests and lure them away from your precious crops. Strong smelling alliums, such as leeks, chives or spring onions, for example, have a scent that deters carrot fly so plant them in staggered rows between the carrots. Leeks, meanwhile, will benefit from the presence of carrots, which will ward off leek moth.

Marigolds are something of a wonder companion plant in the vegetable garden, warding off whitefly from tomatoes, and aphids from beans and brassicas, while attracting slugs away from leafy greens and attracting pollinators to strawberries. Dotted in many of the beds, their bright orange blooms provide pops of colour against the green.

In my garden, using just companion planting and carefully chosen pest-resistant seed varieties, I have no problem growing carrots, spring onions, rocket, cos lettuce, lamb's lettuce, courgettes, tomatoes, potatoes, sweet potatoes, dwarf beans, mangetout, squash, pumpkins, spinach and pak choi.

FRENCH MARIGOLDS

Companion Planting Chart

Plant **SAGE** and **MINT** with **BRASSICAS** to ward off flea beetles (if planting mint in a bed, plant it in a pot to prevent it spreading out of control)

Plant **FRENCH MARIGOLDS** with **TOMATOES** to ward off whitefly

Plant **FRENCH MARIGOLDS** with **RUNNER BEANS**, **FRENCH BEANS** and **BRASSICAS** to ward off aphids and attract ladybirds, lacewings and hoverflies, which prey on aphids

Plant **FRENCH MARIGOLDS** in a ring around **LETTUCE**, **CABBAGE** and **ORIENTAL LEAVES** to attract slugs away from leafy greens

Plant **FRENCH MARIGOLDS** near **STRAWBERRIES** to attract pollinators

Plant **NASTURTIUM** with **BEANS** and **CUCUMBERS** to ward off aphids

Plant **SPRING ONIONS**, **CHIVES** or **LEEKS** with **CARROTS** to ward off carrot root fly

Plant **CARROTS** with **LEEKS** to ward off leek moth

Plant **THYME** or **CHIVES** near **ROSES** to ward off blackfly

But for full protection from the most persistent pests – when growing broccoli and fruit, for example – netting is essential.

Most netting used to cover plants and protect them from birds and flying insects is made of plastic. However, there are biodegradable, plastic-free alternatives out there, which can be sourced with a little searching.

I have only been able to find these alternatives as flat sheets, rather than as ready-made tunnels, but it is easy enough to use canes to fashion a protective covering. Be sure to put overturned pots on top of your canes to avoid risking an eye injury if you bend down to work on the bed.

Wire cloches can be used to protect plants from damage by small animals such as rabbits, free-roaming chickens and squirrels – the latter will often happily

dig up a plant just to see whether they buried a nut underneath it.

TREE PROTECTION

Young trees in rural areas will need protection from deer and other wildlife, who will gnaw at the bark until the tree is no longer able to survive. Most bark guards on the market are plastic, but it is possible now to source ones made of biodegradable water-resistant board.

You can also purchase strips of rubberised coir that can be wrapped around trees, but be careful again with the sourcing, as they are often shipped in plastic packaging.

PLASTIC-FREE NETTING

Dealing With Weeds

Any growing space will have weeds popping up here and there. Their spores or seeds blow in on the wind, or are carried into your growing space by animals and insects. Keeping them at bay is a pleasurable job for some, and a chore for others. For the plastic-free gardener, a more relaxed attitude to sharing your garden with a few unplanned plants goes a long way, so long as the weeds are not invasive types, such as horsetail, knotweed or hogweed.

In the construction of gardens, plastic is used extensively these days, and when creating a new garden it's often a battle to convince landscapers to put aside the polypropylene groundsheets and synthetic membranes. Laid under a path, terrace or gravelled area, the idea is that they form a permanent solution to the problem of weeds growing up through any cracks. It's also a convenient way for the builder to stop the rocks or stones sinking into the earth.

But of course the durability of the plastic membrane is the very problem, particularly when it is literally being built into the natural environment. And as a weed suppressant beneath paths, gravel and patio, they aren't actually that effective because scraps of soil will build up in the cracks, and seeds blown in from above will find themselves a home regardless. Not all weeds come from below.

To clear or reduce the number of weeds on patios, in paths and on the terrace, you can either tug them out by hand, which is easier for some weeds than others; scorch them with a weed torch (though most torches have plastic grips and handles); or spray or coat them with something that will cause them to die. To avoid purchasing weedkiller, which is usually not organic and is always sold in plastic bottles, I use vinegar mixed with a slurp of washing-up liquid (both of which I can source in glass bottles), which I drip or spray onto the most persistent weeds. The others I dig up by hand or just let be.

For beds, some gardeners will put down plastic groundsheet with holes cut out for plants as a low-effort way of keeping weeds at bay. For the plastic-free gardener looking to replicate this, there are biodegradable non-plastic versions on the marketplace made of jute, paper or corn starch. They vary considerably in price, so it's worth shopping around.

Alternatively, you could put down bark (although looking to source it without plastic packaging will have the same complications as compost), or for smaller spaces you can use coir or wool mats, which have the added benefit of acting as a mulch for the soil.

To hand-weed beds, a long-handled hoe is a great tool, slicing through weeds and allowing you to lift the stems in one sweep without bending down. But near precious plants, a hand trowel or

WEEDING WITH A HOE

fork is needed to gently loosen the soil around the weed and allow you to pull it up. Be aware that digging over the soil of a bed to loosen the weeds will bring dormant seeds nearer to the surface and encourage the growth of a wave of new weeds in a week or so.

If you have planted a row of seeds in a vegetable bed, often watering them will encourage other weeds to grow, so when you sow your seeds run a line of string along the row, an inch or two above the soil. When the seeds grow, it will be easier to spot them and not lift them accidentally when weeding the bed.

Gardening Tools

Many tools will have plastic parts, housing the motor of electric tools or connecting moving parts. You also find plastic on handles and forming the small joints of hand tools. It is possible to source manual tools which are entirely plastic-free, but pretty much impossible to source electric devices without plastic, so the plastic-free gardener must choose how far to compromise. Personally, I enjoy clipping a hedge with hand shears, but there are physical and time considerations – an electric hedge trimmer will do the job in a fraction of the time.

As with weeds, it helps if the plastic-free gardener has a slightly more relaxed approach. Many gardeners use a strimmer with a plastic cord to trim the edge of lawns and to strim weeds close to hard or delicate surfaces such as stonework or tree trunks. As strimmers with plastic cords leave minute pieces of plastic in their wake, which are sprinkled into the landscape, they are firmly in the 'ugly' category of plastics in the garden for the plastic-free gardener. Trimming with hand shears instead is possible – but perhaps the better approach, and one that's more in keeping with modern thinking about promoting biodiversity in your garden, is to leave a thin border of longer grass at the edge of the lawn.

If you like to use plastic gloves to protect your fingernails, there are bioplastic versions available, which are designed for use by caterers but work just as well in the garden.

Thinking About Next Year...

Planning ahead makes plastic-free gardening so much easier. Thinking about the following year's planting and growing plan in the current year is a great way to avoid plastic creeping into use in the garden.

FLOWER SEEDS

As the flowers of annuals die, they turn to seed, which can be collected and stored for next year's crop. It's remarkably simple to shake the plant and capture the seeds in envelopes to be stored for the next season, or to let the seeds fall where they will and look out for them when they germinate.

Collected seeds in paper envelopes should be stored in a cool place, where they won't be exposed to high temperatures. A mostly airtight box that can't be nosed into by mice, kept in a porch, shed or garage, is ideal.

Allowing annuals to self-seed in the same bed where there was a particularly good display the previous year is a wonderful plastic-free head start for the next year. Turn the ground over just as the seeds start to send out their first shoots the following spring, as it will encourage other seeds in the soil to germinate. When they have a few leaves, you can thin the seedlings. Either discard those that are too lifted out or, if you remove them gently enough, you can move them to another position in the garden.

Relax and Enjoy

Gardening can be a frustrating hobby at times, and this is doubly true when trying to garden in a plastic-free way – so why do it? To fight the same battles as everyone else is one thing: unexpected late frosts one year, drought the next, foraging raids by hungry deer that eat the head off every tulip you planted in the autumn just as they are about to burst into flower, invasive weeds that seemed under control but suddenly pop up somewhere else, birds picking at the blueberries, mice munching on the strawberries, plants that go rampant and refuse to stay neat, slugs, caterpillars, beetles, rabbits. What a challenge it all is...

Yet the plastic-free gardener has to do it all with added restrictions on the plants, products and tools they can use. They must make do with homemade solutions and inventive cunning. They have to plan ahead even more than other gardeners, growing as much as they can from seed rather than being tempted by the sweet pleasure of a spur-of-the-moment purchase of an exotic plant in a plastic pot. The reality is that they must sometimes face compromise.

But the reward is there. To sit in the garden and enjoy the birdsong, to watch the bees buzzing over the flowers, or to savour a meal made from fresh produce you've grown yourself, all while knowing you are doing your bit to combat plastic pollution – nothing can compare.

HARE SPRING COTTAGE PLANTS

RETAILERS

ONLINE

Cotswold Garden Flowers
https://www.cotswoldgardenflowers.co.uk

A huge range of plant varieties that can be delivered without the pot. Usually offer affordable monthly picks that are easy to grow and care for.

Gee Tee Bulb Company
https://www.gee-tee.co.uk

Based in the heart of Lincolnshire's daffodil-growing region. Has stocked hand-picked flower bulbs from the UK and Netherlands since 1961.

Green Tones
https://www.greentones.co.uk

Stocks brightly coloured bamboo pots ranging from small to larger sizes, along with seed kits.

Hare Spring Cottage Plants
https://www.harespringcottageplants.co.uk

A true plastic-free champion. The nursery grows a wide range of hardy perennials, specialising in Camassia, Sidalcea *and* Uvularia, *and has been completely plastic-free for several years. It tries to make sure even the address labels are plastic-free!*

Harts Nursery
https://www.hartsnursery.co.uk

A third-generation, family run nursery specialising in lilies and other spring- and summer-flowering bulbs, including alliums and tulips. It is happy to ship its bulbs in paper packaging.

H.W. Hyde & Son
https://www.hwhyde.co.uk

Offers bulbs and tubers for a huge selection of gorgeous flowering plants, including many types of lilies and dahlia. A number of the nursery's plants can be sent in paper bags, plastic-free upon request.

Incredible Vegetables
https://www.incrediblevegetables.co.uk

Stocks perennial vegetable plants, seeds and edible tubers following organic and permaculture principles. This is a peat-free nursery and uses cardboard, repurposed newspaper, plant-based bags and paper packing tape for packaging, sending bare-roots plants where possible.

Jacques Amand International
https://www.jacquesamandintl.com

This family business has offered flowering bulbs for over ninety years, beginning as a flower shop in the Strand when Jean Jacques Amand arrived from the Netherlands in 1927. It is able to offer some bulbs in paper packaging.

Kitchen Garden Plant Centre

https://www.kitchengardenplantcentre.co.uk

Another nursery championing the reduction of single-use plastic. This family owned and run nursery grows and offers a fantastic range of herbs and edible plants. As well as being peat- and pesticide-free, it uses recyclable cardboard and biodegradable bags for packaging, and although the plant pots are plastic, all of its pots and plant labels are 100% recyclable.

Paddock Plants

https://www.paddockplants.co.uk

A well-established family run nursery offering a wide range of plants grown peat-free that are delivered with '99% plastic-free packaging', including shrubs, perennials, climbers, grasses and ferns. Its speciality is Indian Mallow.

Pheasant Acre Plants

https://www.pheasantacreplants.co.uk

A family run nursery specialising in the supply of gladioli corms and dahlia tubers and bulbs, some of which can be dispatched plastic-free upon request.

Plastic-Free Gardening

https://www.plasticfreegardening.com

Stocks a number of rubber-free items such as seed markers, twine, metal trays and pots made from coir and rubber, the latter sourced from FSC-certified rubber plantations in Sri Lanka.

The Natural Gardener

https://www.thenaturalgardener.co.uk

A huge range of plastic-replacement products including coir pots and compost discs, troughs, mulch mats and giant jute bags.

Withypitts Dahlias

https://www.withypitts-dahlias.co.uk

A specialist dahlia farm with a reputation for top-quality blooms.

GARDEN CENTRES

Bud Garden Centre

Omer Drive, Burnage, Manchester, M19 2JN

https://www.budgarden.co.uk

Specialises in plants grown in peat-free compost, and offers a compost refill 'bag for life' service.

Burford Garden Centre

Shilton Road, Burford, Oxfordshire, OX18 4PA

https://www.burford.co.uk

A genuine plastic-free hero, worth a day trip for its extensive and carefully sourced range of interior and garden products. It has a huge selection of Hairy Pot Company herbaceous perennials and herbs offered in coir pots, a vast bulb shed (at bulb planting times) with bulbs available in paper bags, and a large selection of jute twine, bamboo pots, seeds and plastic-free gardening tools.

KitchenGarden
PLANT CENTRE

Tel: 07492 903 325
Newent Gloucestershire
www.kitchengardenplantcentre.co.uk

KITCHEN GARDEN PLANT CENTRE

Edible Culture

The Horticultural Unit, The Abbey School, Faversham, Kent, ME13 8RZ

https://www.edibleculture.co.uk

Specialises in selling plants grown peat- and pesticide-free, and without plastic. Its plants are grown from seed, cuttings or young plants, including fruit trees and vines which come from the orchard. It stocks a wide range of edibles including tomato and chilli plants, vegetable seedling plugs, herbs and fruit trees, as well as perennials and shrubs. It also sells tools without plastic, seeds in paper bags, seaweed plant feed in glass bottles and compost in a 'bag for life'. The centre doesn't sell online, but does deliver locally.

Notcutts

https://www.notcutts.co.uk

The company has introduced a range of plastic alternative products including plant pots made from coir, wood fibre, bamboo and bio-based vegetable starch. They stock a wide range of plants from The Hairy Pot Company which use coir pots.

The Plant Centre

Bromfield, Ludlow, Shropshire, SY8 2JR

https://www.ludlowplantcentre.co.uk

The centre is working with its suppliers to move away from bubble wrap in packaging and has never provided plastic bags to customers, using paper bags instead. It does sell plants in plastic pots, but is switching towards recyclable taupe pots.

NURSERIES

Binny Plants

Binny Estate, Ecclesmachan, Uphall, Scotland, EH52 6NL

https://www.binnyplants.com

Offers a vast collection of the most wonderful peonies, plus ferns, grasses and perennials. The nursery works hard to recycle pots within its processes and is happy for customers to return pots after purchasing plants, which the nursery's staff can reuse.

Bluebell Cottage Nursery

Bluebell Cottage, Lodge Lane, Dutton, Nr Warrington, Cheshire, WA4 4HP

https://www.bluebellcottage.co.uk

Specialises in flowering perennials with over 700 plants available, most of which the nursery staff grow from propagating their own stock in peat-free compost, without chemical pesticides. It offers a plastic-free mail-order service, or for visiting customers staff will remove the plastic pot at the counter and wrap the plant in paper; they suggest that you bring a bag to carry it home. For visitors there is a garden with an orchard and wildflower meadow to visit, as well as a tea room.

PlantBase

Sleepers Stile Road, Cousley Wood, Wadhurst, East Sussex, TN5 6QX

http://www.plantbase.co.uk

A wonderfully unique nursery growing 2,080 different varieties of plants, 460 of which are exclusive to its site. Plants range from temperate to tropical, but are all 'born' and 'raised' on site. This means that the plastic used by the nursery is limited – it continually recycles pots in the nursery and is happy for visiting customers to leave the pot of any plants purchased behind for its staff to reuse.

The Coastal Gardener

Fakenham Farm, Eddington Road, St Helens, Isle of Wight, PO33 1XS

https://www.thecoastalgardener.co.uk

Specialises in plants that thrive in maritime conditions, peat-free. Reuses plastic pots.

The Hairy Pot Company

https://www.kirtonfarm.co.uk/stockists

The Hairy Pot Company offers a huge range of quality perennials and herbs sold in coir pots that are distributed via nurseries and garden centres. You can't buy direct from the company, as it sells wholesale only, but the link above gives a full list of the retail outlets that stock its brilliant range of products.

Tissington Nursery

The Old Kitchen Gardens, Tissington, Ashbourne, Derbyshire, DE6 1RA

https://www.tissington-nursery.co.uk

A small family owned nursery in the Peak District National Park, based in the walled old kitchen garden of the Tissington Estate. It grows thousands of plants each year and is happy to facilitate visiting customers leaving the plastic pot behind for reuse.

NOTCUTTS

FOOTNOTES

[1]Thiele, C.J. et al. 'Microplastics in fish and fishmeal: an emerging environmental challenge?', *Nature Scientific Reports*, 11 (2021). doi: 10.1038/s41598-021-81499-8

[2]Kontick, A.V. 'Microplastics and Human Health: Our Great Future to Think About Now', *Journal of Medical Toxicology*, 14(2) (2018), 117–19. doi: 10.1007/s13181-018-0661-9

[3]Kleinschmidt, J.M. and Janosik, A.M. 'Microplastics in Florida, United States: A Case Study of Quantification and Characterization With Intertidal Snails', *Frontiers in Ecology and Evolution*, 9 (2021). doi: 10.3389/fevo.2021.645727

[4]Klein, J.R. et al. 'Microplastics in intertidal water of South Australia and the mussel Mytilus spp.; the contrasting effect of population on concentration', *Science of The Total Environment*, 831 (2022). doi: 10.1016/j.scitotenv.2022.154875

[5]Lofty, J. et al. 'Microplastics removal from a primary settler tank in a wastewater treatment plant and estimations of contamination onto European agricultural land via sewage sludge recycling', *Environmental Pollution*, 304 (2022). doi: 10.1016/j.envpol.2022.119198

[6]Lebreton, L. et al. 'Evidence that the Great Pacific Garbage Patch is rapidly accumulating plastic', *Scientific Reports*, 8(4666) (2018), 1–15. doi: 10.1038/s41598-018-22939-w

[7]Jambeck, J. R. et al. 'Plastic waste inputs from land into the ocean', *Science*, 347(6223) (2015), 768–71. doi: 10.1126/science.1260352

[8]Parker, L. 'The Great Pacific Garbage Patch Isn't What You Think It Is', *National Geographic* (22 March 2018). Available at: https://www.nationalgeographic.com/science/article/great-pacific-garbage-patch-plastics-environment

[9]Chamas, A. et al. 'Degradation Rates of Plastics in the Environment', *ACS Sustainable Chemistry and Engineering,* 8(9) (2020), 3494–511. doi: 10.1021/acssuschemeng.9b06635

[10]Parker, L. 'U.S. generates more plastic trash than any other nation, report finds', *National Geographic* (30 October 2020). Available at: https://www.nationalgeographic.com/environment/article/us-plastic-pollution

[11]McCormick, E. et al. 'Where does your plastic go? Global investigation reveals America's dirty secret', *The Guardian* (17 June 2019). Available at: https://www.theguardian.com/us-news/2019/jun/17/recycled-plastic-america-global-crisis

[12]McVeigh, K. '"Loophole" will let UK continue to ship plastic waste to poorer countries', *The Guardian* (12 January 2021). Available at: https://www.theguardian.com/environment/2021/jan/12/loophole-will-let-uk-continue-to-ship-plastic-waste-to-poorer-countries

[13]Siegle, L. *Turning the Tide on Plastic: How Humanity (And You) Can Make Our Globe Clean Again*. London: Orion, 2018.

[14]CBS Mornings. 'Fast fashion in the U.S. is fueling an environmental disaster in Ghana', *CBS News* (18 September 2021). Available at: https://www.cbsnews.com/news/ghana-fast-fashion-environmental-disaster

[15]Andrady, A.L. and Neal, M.A. 'Applications and societal benefits of plastics', *Philosophical Transactions of the Royal Society of London*, Series B, Biological Sciences, 364(1526) (2009), 1977–84. doi:10.1098/rstb.2008.0304

[16]WWF. 'The lifecycle of plastics', *WWF* (19 June 2019). Available at: https://www.wwf.org.au/news/blogs/the-lifecycle-of-plastics

[17]Appleby, M. 'Time for Government action on plastic plant pot recycling, say horticulture industry figures', *Horticulture Week* (13 November 2018). Available at: https://www.hortweek.com/time-government-action-plastic-plant-pot-recycling-say-horticulture-industry-figures/ornamentals/article/1498930

IMAGES

Copyright

The Plastic-Free Gardener
First published by Fairlight Books 2024

Fairlight Books
Summertown Pavilion, 18–24 Middle Way, Oxford, OX2 7LG

A CIP catalogue record for this book is available from the British Library

ISBN 978-1-914148-55-2

www.fairlightbooks.com

Printed and bound in Czech Republic by Finidr

Book and cover design by Rebecca Fish

MIX
Paper | Supporting responsible forestry
FSC® C014138